7 DAYS AND 11 NIGHTS

How to Write a Novella for the Digital Age

by Jack Lehman

Zelda Wilde Publishing

Jack Lehman

Text copyrighted 2014 by John Lehman

The cover image is copyrighted by the Wikimedia Foundation and used with their approval.

ISBN-13: 978-0615799162
ISBN-10: 0615799167

DEDICATION

Dedicated to my favorite "here and now" writer, the poet Richard Brautigan.

Jack Lehman

7 Days and 11 Nights

CONTENTS

Day One – Not Setting Goals 9

Night One – Kim Kong 13

Night Two – Peripheral Vision

Day Two – "You're Fired" 35

Night Three – Little Death 41

Night Four – Three Notes 51

Day Three – Meaning 61

Night Five – A Strange Claim

Night Six – Ghosts 79

Day Four – Lunch 89

Night Seven – Hermitage 95

Night Eight – Possibilities 105

Day Five – We Are Story 113

Night Nine – Underground Man

Night Ten – Grace 131

Day Six – Truth 143

Night Eleven – Epilogue 147

Day Seven – But Not Least

About the Author 155

Jack Lehman

just
when the
caterpillar
thought the
world was
over, it
became a
butterfly

- a proverb

Day One – Not Setting Goals

Jack Lehman

Why are we obsessed with goals and achieving goals?

Perhaps that is why you are reading this book. There is a promise in the sub-title that implies I will show you how to write a novella and that by accomplishing this (in the digital age) you will achieve success that makes you happy.

"Eat your Wheaties and you'll grow up to be a sports champion." "Pay attention in class and you will get a good grade on the semester exam." "Work hard and you will be promoted to assistant manager in no time." "He had a difficult life, but now he is enjoying heaven."

From birth to death we are immersed in expectations and in seeking simple formulas to achieve them. What we want is…certainty. That's not what we get.

Writing, real writing, is a wonderful metaphor. Whether writing or reading, we can grasp a significance for us that changes as we do. That's what I want to communicate to you in this book. You already have the tools, you already have all the experiences you need to draw upon, you already have the intuition to see below the surface of things. What you need is the opportunity to bring these into focus and the encouragement to know this will work and bring you more fulfillment than any, ANY, false expectations ever did.

Let's look at the process.

You sit down with a blank legal pad or stare at an empty computer screen. You are here and now.

Whatever characters (real or imagined) fill out the scene have to react to one another. Even if you recount something that happened to you years ago, to make it real and immediate, each has to have something he or she wants to accomplish, be doing something and experience some emotion on the page or on the computer screen. Like a reader, you are writing to find out what will happen (and even if you are recording an actual incident, this one will be different because you are different and because the insight you have into each of the people will be different from when it happened). Like God, there is an intensity of bringing something from nothing, that is more real than conversation over the dinner table or plans for next summer's vacation.

When it is over...but it is never over. Finishing a novella, getting it published are incidental to the real rush of the living thing. It means every person you meet, every place you go, every dilemma you face is material for the real show.

"There are no magicians, only great actors who play magicians," Orson Welles said, "who perform hypnosis on a small scale that causes us to fall asleep into other worlds."

A great writer is also a great actor who causes readers, editors, teachers and most important, himself or herself, to enter, not another world, but the one we now inhabit in a trance like state.

And sitting at your computer in the dark, know the curtain is parting. Hear applause start. Feel the spotlight.

Don't think. Start!.

Here are the first two chapters of my novella, *Geography of Sleep*, I came up with when I did that.

Night One – Kim Kong

Jack Lehman

Chapter 1

Kim Kong

My name is Max Jordan. At the time this all started I was working for a guy who didn't know what he was doing. How am I *sure*? Because he was an English major like me. At one point he had decided it might be fun to go into business. He'd done some cartoons for a local weekly paper and thought maybe he could do illustrations for ads that appeared there. So my future boss contacted the area business magazine and they sent a man out to his house (he didn't have an office). The reporter took a picture of him sitting in a rocking chair. The owner of a small adhesives company saw the picture and hired him to do their ads. The name of that company, "Broken Rocker." Later Charles Nash discovered that this man was also partners in a large building-materials manufacturing firm. After they "bonded," a term Charlie liked to use in retelling the glue story, he was given the opportunity to do some trade-magazine ad production and placement. That's when he decided he would have to learn how to do the job they wanted, or hire some people who claimed they could. But two clients weren't enough to justify a staff so he hired me as an account executive to bring in new business and service existing clients. My only qualifications: I had gone to the same college as he did

One of those new accounts had a young Asian American receptionist I was particularly attracted to. She possessed the incredible name "Kim Kong," was small, sweet, divorced and had an eight-year old, mildly autistic daughter. She also had the kind of laugh that reminded me of a wind chime in a gentle breeze. I knew her as an associate before Carolyn and I split up. Now we had gone on several innocent dates and one not so innocent one. I called her from the office later one morning to tell Kim I had discovered the manuscript of a mystery story my two aunts had written. I said that after my Aunt Babe's recent death (Flora had passed on years earlier), I had looked everywhere for it, then, a few days ago, it mysteriously appeared stuck between my front door and the storm.

"That is so strange," she squealed, "how could anyone know you were looking for that manuscript?"

She sounded like something out of Nancy Drew. I loved it.

Lowering my voice I answered, "I don't know, Miss Kong, but do you believe in… the supernatural."

She laughed.

"So when do we get together to read it?" I asked.

"You want me to look at it too?"

"Of course, Kim. It's you and me. Together we can figure out anything."

"Maybe," she replied, but she sounded suspicious of my motives.

When we met for a bag lunch at a Forest Preserve half-way

between her company and the agency, the early spring was warm enough for a short walk. There was the promise of better weather ahead. But, being Chicago, this also meant the possibility of setbacks—like freak snow, an inexplicable cold week or, at minimum, a thundershower that for a few minutes would turn to bouncing hail.

"So tell me about your Aunt Flora," she asked.

"Well she taught handicapped kids for forty years. Once, when I was young, I went with her for a day. The students were all different ages and grades. Mostly I remember spilled chocolate milk, broken cloak room hooks and her sitting in front of the class at her desk straightening papers.

"Those were the days when they had the special-needs children in separate classes from the regular kids."

"Not only in separate classes," I added, "but in entirely different schools."

"Was she kind to the children?" Kim was thinking how people treated her own daughter.

"I don't know. Remember I was pretty young myself. I think she kept them busy and was respectful. But she never seemed to me to be a person who was particularly kind."

"And do you recall anything else about her?"

"Just incidental things. She had an old fashioned dress-form in the attic. A wonderful two-person swing on her front porch. Her house always smelled of boiled cabbage. She would usually be wearing some kind of housecoat when I saw her and, oh yes, along the back fence, where the garbage cans were lined up near the alley, there was a row of these great, tall hollyhocks."

"Nice."

We were sitting in my old, 1970 Cadillac Coup de Ville by this time. Kim was eating a tuna fish sandwich she had made, and I munched down a couple of burgers I'd purchased at MacDonald's on the way over here.

"When I was in the Army, after Aunt Flora had retired, my mom wrote about going over to her house. Flora was in bed, layered in clothes eating dinner from cans. My aunt once had a roommate. I don't know what had happened to her. She must have been elderly by then too and perhaps went to live with her nieces in Milwaukee. Eventually they took Aunt Flora north to a nursing home in Upper Michigan, The Apple Orchard, where she spent her last days. My mother said she heard one of the other occupants there refer to Flora as 'a lady from Chicago.'"

"That's sad. And have you read any of the manuscript yet."

"Not really. I glanced at the dedication, and I did discover how it got to me," I added this last little bit of information to ally Kim's suspicions.

"How?"

"Zachery, her attorney. He had visited Babe in the hospital to review her will and she must have given it to him with instructions that he was to send it or deliver it to me."

"OK."

"My guess is that he dropped it off early on his way to work."

"Well that's one mystery solved," she said and grinned. "And who is the manuscript dedicated to."

Kim wasn't at all like the mighty gorilla that climbed the Empire State Building whose name hers reminded me of. She was just the opposite. Sitting there, wide faced, almond eyes, cropped black hair. She was quite a bit younger than I was, and looking at her now she seemed just a girl, and I someone who had spent too much time in college, too much time in the Army, too much time in graduate studies. I didn't know if I was in love with her, but she certainly represented a part of life that I had missed and wanted to reclaim.

"Some guy named 'Harry Davidson,'" I said. "I never heard the name before. I assume it was someone in Rockdale who lived there when they did."

"Max, here's what you should do? You know those things that pop up on the Internet when you sign in for E-Mail, 'Find a Classmate?'"

"Yeah, sure."

"You just plug in his name and see what comes up. Maybe with the high school graduation dates of your aunts. Do you know when each graduated."

"No, but I think I can figure out the dates."

"Great."

This was an interesting idea. I knew Kim thought it might be fun to do this together but Kim was dedicated to her daughter. She went to work an hour early so she could be there when the school bus dropped Liviana off in the afternoon. The two of them would look at picture books (always the same ones) and prepare a simple dinner together. Afterwards they went to bed around nine and snuggled until falling asleep. But on Saturdays, and sometimes Sundays, the daughter spent time with her father. It was at this time Kim suggested we could meet at a local coffee shop, "Cool Plums" and start to read a chapter or two of my aunts' book. I knew the place. It had cushy leather couches and fat, overstuffed chairs. Afterward she promised I could come over and she would cook some fresh trout for dinner.

When I returned to the office my boss, Charlie Nash, called me into his little room and shut the door.

"I'm afraid I have some bad news for you," he began.

I stared at him in disbelief. "What's that?" I asked.

"Well business has been slow, the economy you know, and I have to make some cuts. I can't let any of the graphic artists or the computer guy go because they are servicing accounts that do pay. But, temporarily anyway, I have to dismiss you, Max. You've done a good job. I can't think of anything you could have done differently, and I like you, I really do. But…"

"It's all right, Charlie, I understand," I replied, to save him more embarrassment.

"You could work on commission-only if you like, but you'd probably make more drawing unemployment. It's up to you. And, of course, if things start to open up again, I want you back."

"Thanks, I appreciate that." I rose from my chair.

"Are you OK, Max? Really. I mean will you be able to get by?"

The interior of this 50's, one-story building with parking around back suddenly seemed generic and dull. This scene of losing a job I didn't want had a dreamlike quality to it that I was passive to. Charlie was nervous. He was uncomfortable letting someone go. He had to make changes and he was anxious to move on. As soon as the "old" was out the door they could all tell themselves bad times were behind them. And maybe they were. The reality was I didn't care.

"I'll think of something. Please, don't worry about me, Charlie. Keep this place hopping," I said with a wink and a smile.

As a matter of fact I had already thought of something while he was talking. Unemployment compensation would probably cover rent on my Jonquil Terrace apartment and my monthly car insurance. I didn't really have any savings, but there would be money coming in from Aunt Babe's estate. Even if I had to live off credit cards for a short while, I'd be all right. And what I wanted was not to find a different job or even a better one, but to take some time and sort through my life. In a way this was a gift.

We shook hands and I told him I needed about ten days to tie things up. He said I should take my time. Just as my separation from Carolyn had been a chance at a new start, now I had another. Thanks to Aunt Babe, this was almost exciting.

Before I left that night, I later told Kim, I typed the name "Harry Davidson"' into one of those "Where are they now" sites. "Davidson" proved to be a popular name and it was only after I added a plus sign and "Rockdale, WI" that I found what I was looking for.

It looked like an obituary notice that might have appeared in the *Cambridge News* (Cambridge, Wisconsin, I knew was the largest town near Rockdale. Rockdale had a population of a little over 200, Cambridge's was about 1,200).

I don't know what I'd expected to find. Perhaps that he was a teacher at my aunts' high school or a coach of some kind. Maybe a neighbor who had befriended them, encouraged their writing, bought them notebooks.

> Davidson, Harry, 1948 – unknown, member of the Cambridge H.S. class of 1966. Mysteriously went missing two months before graduation. At the time thought to have left the state. His body was recovered ten years later by workers in the quarry outside of Rockdale. Police suspected foul play. Survived by his younger sister, Penelope, and older brothers Tom and Hank. Posthumous services were held by the family at the Koshkonong Lutheran Church where Harry Davidson's remains were buried. Friends remembered the young Davidson as being athletic, affable and very popular among teachers and friends.

Perhaps this was my aunts tribute to a departed classmate. But their story was written fifty or sixty years later. Would he still have had such emotional impact upon them after all that time. I doubted it. By then they would have been transplanted to Chicago, involved in very different worlds of very different people, unless he somehow had played a part in their story. Were that the case, their fictional tale was grounded in something that had actually happened. If Kim and I could delve beneath the surface we might still be able to discover what that was.

I couldn't wait for Saturday when we would begin together.

Jack Lehman

Night Two – Peripheral Vision

Jack Lehman

Chapter 2

Peripheral Vision

When I fell asleep slightly after midnight, I dreamt not about Harry Davidson or my aunts, but that I was driving along a two-lane road out in the country. It must have been early spring because there were no leaves on the branches of clumps of trees and I could see the hills with their recently tilled rows of earth silhouetted behind them. The highway would dip down and then rise up to intersections with their metal sheds or old tobacco barns. It was mid-afternoon and this, I realized, was Wisconsin. I heard the moan of a distant freight train and felt some impending disaster awaited me. Kim was beside me in the car, but asleep against the window on the passenger side.

"Kim," I whispered in the dream. There was no response. Her peach colored eyelids were closed. "Kim," I repeated, "wake up." Then I tapped her shoulder gently with my right hand. I had meant this as a nudge, but when she didn't wake I pushed harder against her. That's when I realized she wasn't sleeping. She was dead.

In the morning I called Kim.

"Are you all right?" I asked.

"Sure," she replied, "why wouldn't I be?"

"Oh, I had a nightmare about you last night and it was so realistic I just wanted to phone and check."

"I'm fine, you silly. Now I have to go. I'm getting Liviana ready for school and the oatmeal is boiling over on the stove. See you Saturday. And no more bad dreams!"

I took out an old road atlas I had in the hall closet and traced the route from Chicago to Madison and then over to the Cambridge/Rockdale area. I wanted Kim and I to look at the story first, but I felt that the dream I'd had was some kind of premonition. After we'd read the manuscript I would drive to Wisconsin and examine those hills and crossroads for myself.

Saturday ended up being more complicated than we had planned. The evening before, Liviana had had a seizure. Saturday morning Kim had wanted to be sure the girl was really OK before letting Liviana's father pick her up for an afternoon and over-night stay.

Kim called me and canceled our meeting. Then she called an hour later and asked if we could simply reschedule it for later. That meant we wouldn't be having dinner or that I might not be staying over. Compared to losing my job this seemed a minor set-back. To be honest, after my traumatic dream, I was glad we were getting together under any circumstances. I wanted to see her, touch her, hear her voice.

For you see I do believe in dreams. Oh, not literally. I don't think they can predict the future, for example; but, in some subtle way, there is something more to them than most people realize. They are like peripheral vision. And if we examine the incidental things in dreams, not those that seem to be the center of attention, they can offer some clues to truth below the surface, not of the dream, but below the surface of our lives. The same is true for movies or novels or even poetry. "Tell the Truth but tell it slant," Emily Dickenson wrote in one of her pieces. So it is the time of year within the dream or its particular setting or the shadows that are or are not there that matter. I call this the "geography of sleep." The significance of my nightmare may not have been Kim but the potholes in the road. However there was some significance somewhere. That's why when faced with a difficult situation or I'm searching for a clarification of some kind, I will often close my eyes and go to sleep. When I awake, what I have been looking for is there.

I picked Kim up at 4pm on Saturday. She seemed distracted.

"How's Liviana," I asked thinking that this was the problem.

"Oh, she's fine. I mean she was OK this morning but I asked her dad to bring her back tonight instead of her staying with him."

"Good," I said, but was hoping for better.

"It's you I'm concerned about," she said looking over at me as I tried to parallel park in a small space down the block from the coffee shop.

"What do you mean? I'm fine."

"Are you?" she scrunched her nose. "You lose your job, call me about having nightmares, obsess over your aunts' manuscript."

"How did you know I lost my job?"

"Charles Nash told my boss, and Mel told me…or I should say he told all of us."

"Well, Charlie is experiencing a downturn in business, and he has to cut corners a bit," I said.

"That's not what he told Mel."

"I looked at her after opening the door on her side of the car. We walked over to Cool Plums. A whiff of espresso greeted us at the door.

I imagined that Charlie couldn't tell clients he was in financial trouble, but I did wonder what kind of a story he would tell about letting me go.

Kim took off her jacket and slid into a booth. Vivaldi was playing softly in the background. This was not a busy time of day. Older patrons had gone home, the younger Wy-FI crowd were off on their plans for a Saturday night. I placed the manuscript on the table and took off my Navy Pea coat. There were framed posters from old movies on the wall: *To Have and Have Not, Death in Venice, Invasion of the Body Snatchers*.

"So what did Mel say Charlie told him about me?" I asked as we looked over the menus.

"He said that because of problems with your wife you had not been able to concentrate on the job. That you needed some time to regroup. That you were a disappointment."

"He said I was a disappointment?"

"I'm sorry, Max, I don't mean to be hurtful but that is what he did say."

"Oh."

"And I think it better that you know what is being said about you, don't you?"

I suddenly felt that the wind had been knocked out of me. "Do you think I'm a disappointment, Kim?"

"What. Of course not." she reached over and took my hand.

I just wasn't sure what to think. Why would Charlie go that far? In fact why would Kim even tell me this? I had felt I was reaching out to her. Offering some support and love to someone who not only found herself alone but had the added responsibility of raising an autistic child. Liviana was a nice little girl but emotionally distant. Kim would have to care for her the daughter's entire life. She seemed to accept this but it couldn't be easy. Or was she one of those people who seemed destined to care for others? For her daughter? For me?

"So have you ever been to Rockdale?" she asked, obviously trying to change the subject.

"Only once, when I was about your Liviana's age," I replied.

"Tell me about it," she smiled.

"To be honest, what I remember best was our stopping at a

shopping mall on the way back and going to a James Bond movie. It was so out of character for my dad to ever stop anywhere, even for a bathroom break, and here we were on the way home to Chicago going to a theater in the middle of the afternoon. Sean Connery was Bond."

"You went with your parents, then?"

"My father wanted to go to Rockdale. He also was from there. Some kind of pottery festival was going on in Cambridge at a park on Lake Ripley. But I think mostly he just wanted to drive around. My mother hated it. They ended up having an argument the final morning and that's why we were driving back home to Chicago early. Neither of them wanted to see a movie, really, but I think they felt they owed it to me."

"Why did your father like visiting their hometown and your mother didn't?"

"I really don't know. Well, maybe I do have some idea."

"What?"

"My father was a Presbyterian, at least that's what he put on any papers he filled out that had a box for religion, and my mother and her sisters and mother were all Catholic. In those days people of different religions didn't date or get married to one another."

"But your parents did?"

"After they both had moved to Chicago. And in this city no one cared. But returning to their roots was somehow embarrassing for my mom. At least that's my guess. I was about eight and really don't remember specifics of the trip. Other than the movie and spending the night in an old fashioned motel outside of Cambridge. Oh, yeah, and we had roast beef at a restaurant Saturday night."

"But didn't you say your mother and her sisters weren't that close."

"No, they weren't. How about you? Don't you have a brother, and what about your parents?" I asked, hoping for some background from Kim. But she didn't answer me. The coffee had arrived and a piece of cherry cheesecake we had agreed to share.

Gusts of wind were blowing rain against the outside window. Where had that come from? For a moment we both were quiet, eating the desert and drinking our big cups of rich coffee. I had told her about the obituary I'd found, and we'd gone over the first two chapters of my aunts' *Swimming by the Cemetery*. I read the first out loud to her and then she did the same with the second to me. We talked about them a bit on the drive to her place.

It was curious. The story was well written. It had obviously gone through several revisions and this was a polished draft. Somehow I thought the characters would be older, probably because I saw my aunts as adults, not as high school age. I had expected more dynamics between the two collaborators—maybe one putting something down and challenging the other to respond to it in a meaningful way. There didn't seem to be that kind of tension. But more than anything else, I realized as Kim and I were doing this together that to understand what was at the heart of the relationship between Flora, Babe and this boy named Harry Davidson, I would need to somehow also grasp the connection between Kim, Carolyn and myself . I know that sounds crazy, but I was sure that was the case; and the way Kim looked at me when we finished, I knew she felt the same way.

Traffic started to pick up on Clark Street as Kim and I headed back. After all, it was Saturday night. The rain had stopped. I checked my mail inside the front door of the apartment then headed around back to take the grey outside stairs up to the third floor. A cat ran out from behind the garbage can on the second floor landing. It scuttled down as I continued up. But I did pause at the top of the steps before opening my kitchen door. I looked out over the back yards and alleys. Now the dark sky was full of stars. I felt like I was in the crow's nest of an old ship looking out over the sea, glancing toward the heavens to see if I was on course.

Kim called me later that night. Liviana had had another seizure after returning home. "She's in bed, sleeping," the worried mother sighed.

Day Two – "You're Fired"

Jack Lehman

There are two things that immediately pleased me about the first chapter of my novella. First, the firing. Not because I am cruel, on the contrary, I have not only been fired but have had to fire other people and I think the second is harder. I remember once a guy who worked for me at my graphic studio stayed on vacation a couple weeks beyond what he had told us and that put our business and several of the people who worked for me in a perilous position. When I told him that he was fired, Spencer turned to me and said, "Will I still get a going away party?" He did and went on to do some exciting book covers, including one for a book of my poetry through Cambridge Book Review Press.

No, I met someone in the Army when I was in Germany, George Rabito, who had been a business consultant in civilian life. One night, over a few beers, he told me, "Everyone should get fired at least once. You will never be caught off guard again." And I remembered being fired from my position as executive officer in Vietnam. And how, working my way into a battalion headquarters position of adjutant/personnel officer, I was able to stand-by and not prevent that old commanding officer from being sent to a small infantry unit at the front. Revenge is sweet, but it was more than that. Never before did I get caught off guard again. And sometimes those instances of disappointment become the kick in the butt to do something I should but needed a push to begin a new journey. Like starting a literary magazine or writing books.

That brings me to the belief that things are neither good nor bad. We may see them as one thing at the time, but later credit it as providing us with a new direction with which to achieve a more-fulfilling happiness.

To me that's also the difference between the short story and a novella. A short story suggests change whereas a novella can probe nuances of the results (as opposed to a novel where we lose ourselves in another world, in other characters, and in a plot that is self contained).

But there's more. Max and Kim are brought together through their investigation of a manuscript by Max's aunts. They are looking for clues below the surface, as I hope readers of the story are wondering what is really going on. It is a play within a play. And as a writer this sort of metaphysical perspective allows me to think about what I am doing, or trying to do. In the end I come up with something: 1) satisfying to my characters, 2) satisfying to the reader by speaking directly to what he or she is actively involved with, and 3) satisfying to me because I am immersed in a creative process which lets me deal with problems and people in a fictionalized way that puts me in control and gives me a catharsis that encourages me to do even more of this in the future.

As the plot of the manuscript unfolds, we also see Max is trying to redeem himself. It is no longer just that he has time to do this—thanks to unemployment payments and his aunt's inheritance—but that his former boss and clients have judged him as incompetent.

The cards are dealt. The stakes are getting higher. And the game is here and now! On to the next two chapters of *Geography*

7 Days and 11 Nights

of Sleep.

Jack Lehman

Night Three – Little Death

Jack Lehman

Chapter 3

Little Death

Here is how Flora Stand's and Babe O'Reilly's *Swimming by the Cemetery* begins:

There are faces of ghosts at my window. Outside the old rocking chair creaks in the wind. I can't sleep. I keep thinking about my sister and Harry. When I close my eyes all I can see are moonlight and black rocks. What have I done.

We live on a hill in Rockdale, a village of 200 people, my mother, my older sister Ruth, Barbara and me. Barb and I are only a year apart. She is graduating from high school in a week and I am going to be a senior. My father, August, passed away from tuberculosis shortly after I was born. He had been a tobacco farmer, made good money, then died. Now there are the four of us. A house of women.

Our home was built in 1859 and originally was a stage coach stop between Madison and Milwaukee. There had been a tavern in the basement, a dor- like sleeping room upstairs and private quarters for the Nelsons, the original owners, on the second floor. The old brick building with its flowering crab trees, lilac bushes and pines is across the road from the Koshkonong River. "Koshkonong" was an Ojibwa term meaning, "where there is heavy fog."

Now the basement is a musty catch-all of boxes and old

Christmas decorations. The first floor became a living room, dining room and kitchen. Mama has the bedroom to the front at the top of the stairs. Ruth has a tin-ceiling one across from her, and Barb and I share a knotty pine room across the back (it was an addition put on thirty years ago that enclosed the rear stairs and added a bathroom to the upstairs). Cambridge, where Barb and I attend high school, is two miles or an interminable school bus ride north of here.

Barb and I first got involved with Harry in a creative writing class. We were there because we wanted to be novelists. He, on the other hand, needed an English credit to graduate and this looked like an easy way to get it.

Mr. Larson's initial instructions were typically vague: "Work together in groups of three to five. Come up with a project for the semester that shows creativity. Half of each of your grade will be based on the outcome."

The class of 17 easily formed into small work units, That is, except for Barb, Harry and me. We were like the odd table at a wedding reception of individuals no one wanted to talk with. So we decided to work together. Harry immediately asked Mr. Larson if we could leave the classroom to brainstorm. The teacher was as anxious to be rid of us as our classmates. He probably thought we would go to the library, but instead Harry led us to the bench outside the building that was in front of the guidance office windows. It was a sunny day and we didn't need our jackets. The bench faced an expanse of grass in front of the high school. It was green from the frequent rain of the last few weeks. There were some lilies and tulips already up around the secondary entrance to the building behind us. But mostly it was dandelions, and a carpet of green before us freckled with their patches of yellow. Our mother would be working in the vegetable garden at home.

"How about this," Barb began as Harry pulled out a cigarette and lit it. "We could write a play about two sisters during the Civil War, one married to someone from the North the other to a Confederate."

"Naw," Harry dismissed the idea. "Larson would want us to put it on, and I'm just not in the mood for that."

"Well, then what are you in the mood for," I shot back, a little annoyed that we had to be anchored to this second-string jock.

"Dunno," he exhaled and winked at Barb.

"How about some kind of a travelogue or documentary on Cambridge and Rockdale," I offered knowing Harry wasn't going to write anything.

"You know, my dad's got an old super-8 camera."

"We could film historic settings and there could be a voice-over telling about them," I added.

"Here's a better idea," he replied, and then he said nothing. Barb and I looked at Harry. He seemed to be thinking over his plan. You could almost see the gear-wheels of his brain slowly turning.

"What, for crying out loud?" Barb finally said.

"Did you ever see the Monty Python stuff on TV?" he asked.

"Yeah...," we both answered.

"This sounds kind of nutty, but I think that approach could work for us."

"Go on," I said.

"Well, I'll be the director."

"Of course," I added sarcastically.

"And, Dora, you can be the cameraman."

All of a sudden this was sounding interesting. He stood up, and, cigarette in his mouth, talked rapidly waiving his hands.

"It will begin with Barb in a desk in the Creative Writing class. It's as if she's thinking about other places. And then we see her in her desk going down the sidewalk."

"What" Barb objected. "And how exactly do I go down a sidewalk in a school desk?"

Harry took the cigarette from his mouth, threw it to the ground, and, for dramatic effect, twisted the stub into the grass with the toe of his right shoe. "That's where Monty Python comes in. We do it with stop action photography. You're in the desk, we pull the trigger on the camera for a second, you get out of the desk, we inch it forward. You get back in, we pull the camera trigger for *another second or two, and so on..."*

We both looked at him. He took a little bow and plopped back down on the bench beside Barb.

"I think it could work," I said in amazement.

"We could have a sequence at the bakery and even down by the lake," Barb added.

"And listen to this for a finish," Harry exclaimed as we heard the bell ring ending class inside the building. "Down on the railroad tracks. Barb will start with her back near the camera and gradually go off down the line into the distance. Maybe we can record a sound track with a Willy Nelson song or something for the ending."

There it was. Later that week I would go over to Harry's house and he'd give me the movie camera with an instruction book (he had never used it himself). His father was fine with the idea since it was for school and his son had never shown enthusiasm for any of his classes in the past. In the basement was also a two-wheel thing for slowly looking at the movie, frame by frame. The film could then be cut and spliced together with a special clear tape in whatever order we wanted it. I was going to learn to shoot movies and then be able to edit them. And, of course, there was also a projector. None of this involved sound, but we could record music on a tape recorder later. Harry's idea was good for that too, since there would be no dialogue which we would've had to coordinate with the picture.

The rest of the week in the Creative Writing class the three of us discussed different possible locations. Harry had an old van we could use, though we couldn't leave the school grounds during the day so would have to do much of the filming on weekends.

"I love the way he swaggers around," Barb said to me as we lay in our beds one night. "He's so thin and sexy," she added.

Maybe, but I also thought there was something suspicious about him. And, as it turned out, I was the one he had his eye on.

It happened one night after dinner when I was down in his basement alone editing the first roll that had been developed at the drugstore. I loved the process. I would cut strips of the film and tack them up to hang down from the side of the table with little pieces of masking tape. The trick was remembering which was which. Harry's family was upstairs watching television. I could hear the sound from a sitcom through the floor. There was the smell of fried chicken in the house. I couldn't remember what we'd had for dinner a half hour before.

I slowly turned the hand crank that pulled the film to the new real. The room where I was working was used for some kind of storage. It was completely dark except for the little half-inch lighted frame. My right eye was no more than a finger's width away from it. Suddenly I felt Harry's presence behind me. I hadn't heard the door open or close, nor did he say anything. I straightened up and turned around. All I could see was the black outline of his finger in front of his mouth and hear him whisper, "shhhh."

I started to say something about the film or his family or the house. Instead he wrapped his arms around me and pressed his lips against my mouth.

I had never kissed a boy before. I was tense, wondering what Barb would think if she knew. He moved back a few inches and told me to relax. I did. He kissed me again, and this time I kissed him back.

There were many evenings like this. It was exciting. I had a convenient excuse to be out at night, even to be in his home. He was taking advantage of this too. Perhaps rewarding me for helping him graduate. Or was it that he genuinely liked me and found me somehow attractive. I didn't know, and to be honest I didn't care. There would be twenty minutes of kissing, and sometimes his hand would wander down my back toward the curve to my butt, and then he'd leave. In public there was not contact. If no one was looking, he or I might smile at the other. And once he turned in class and caught me staring at him. Barb suspected nothing. In fact, during the shooting, she would be coquettish with him. And Harry would play along.

We filmed a sequence at the bakery/café. We had some classmates act as customers since the stop-action technique took hours for a few minutes results and we had to have those in the background remain perfectly still while we rearranged the desk. We did the same at the bank, and late one Saturday afternoon I filmed Barb going into and coming out of the shallow water at the beach. It was hilarious, partly because the water was still freezing cold. But she did it. We did it. Somehow it was like we were in the movie business. This wasn't a student film, it was our launch *toward Hollywood. For once the other kids in the school were jealous of Barb and me.*

Then there was the morning we went to the rock quarry. Just outside of Rockdale. It was no Grand Canyon. Some of the stone from it was used to decorate the main street and traffic circle in the village. This particular morning was foggy and cold. I went back to the van up above to get my jacket. Harry grabbed Barb and gave her a long French kiss. They didn't know I had returned down the trail. They didn't know I had seen them.

Night Four – Three Notes

Jack Lehman

Chapter 4

Three Notes

The next chapter of the manuscript continues on where the first one left off. As Kim and I read this it wasn't clear at this point that both aunts had actually written it. Since it seemed to be from Flora's point of view, Kim thought this was all her work. I suggested that Babe could have been projecting what happened on to her sister in which case this was all her writing. After all, she had wanted me to read it. In either case whoever wrote it would have affected the truth of the piece. Not the truth of the story, but of our interpretation of the reality it was based upon.

The next evening, over at Harry's house, I stayed a little later editing than I usually did. There was the passionate interlude, but when I went upstairs to the kitchen later it was empty. I saw some school books and a thin-lined notebook on the counter that Harry must have carelessly left there when he came home from school that day. I couldn't imagine he ever did any homework, but he wasn't above pretending that he did.

I listened carefully, then stole across the room and quietly ripped four sheets of paper out of the back of the notebook. This was exactly what I needed.

That day at the quarry I pretended I hadn't seen anything, and since this was consistent with what they wanted to believe, I was OK. My job would not be that difficult. It wasn't that I had to imitate Harry's handwriting, but rather I needed to give the impression I was him disguising his lettering so it wouldn't be recognized. The rest was simple. Put an anonymous note in an envelope addressed to my sister and make it look like someone had stuck it into our locker. Here's what I wrote in left-handed scrawl:

> Barb, I know about you and Harry. If you don't want me to tell your sister it will cost you $20. Put the money in an envelop Tuesday and leave it at the base of the stop sign exiting the high school parking lot before lunch. – A Friend

I purposely misspelled "envelop." I was a genius. Tuesday before class I grabbed Husky Hartman, an overweight sophomore girl in my Spanish class.

"Listen, Husky, I'll give you five bucks, enough to buy desert for a week, if you'll do a really confidential favor for me.

"Five bucks?"

"Sure. You see I overheard my sister talking on the telephone to a boyfriend last night. He's going to drop off a letter for her. Probably a love letter. Anyway, I want you to get it for me. If it's not sealed I'll read it and give it to her, pretending I didn't look at it. If it is sealed I'll just give it to her later tonight. But listen. Whatever you do, I don't want her to know about this plan, understand? Go out at lunch. "

"And what am I to do with the envelope? I mean, how do I get it to you?"

"Slip it to me in Spanish class this afternoon and I'll give you the money then."

She didn't. Instead while Barb and I were eating lunch in the cafeteria Husky came up to me and said a little too excitedly, "Here's that magazine I said you could borrow" and gave me some junky girl's magazine with, I knew, the envelope tucked inside. She wasn't all that smooth, and neither was I, but Barb was preoccupied and didn't seem to notice anything out of the ordinary. Later I gave the sophomore her $5 and, of course, I would keep the envelope with the money.

That was the first note. Barb never suspected it was supposedly from Harry. I did go out of my way at one point to say how unusual it was that Harry used a notebook with lines so close together, as if he were already a college student or something. She nodded her head and didn't make the connection to the anonymous letter on the same kind of paper.

The second note was a bit more menacing. I wanted him to appear more of a threat, and one that she would have difficulty dealing with except, of course, with my help. Here is what it said:

> Barb, I know you know this is from me. I am in serious financial trouble. I can't tell my parents. I really need your help. You must believe I love you. I want to have sex with you tonight. Meet me at Heather's Grill around 8pm. I have a plan. But without you I'm lost. Harry

I started six of the nine sentences with "I." If that didn't sound like Harry I don't know what would. But here was the insidious part of my scheme. I would go over to Heather's myself and make Barb feel that he knew I was there so he couldn't risk meeting her. She'd know that, one way or another, she would have to confide in me. We ate our family dinner around six. Barb proved more quiet than usual. She said she had school work to do and a little before eight told our mom she was going out for a walk.

I said nothing, but left the house a few minutes after she did. I walked down the street to Heather's. It was just a bar really, a hangout for motorcycle guys and hollow-eyed farmhands who were single and had no place better to go. The place was known for three things: cheap draft beer, really juicy hamburgers and Heather's was lax on checking IDs.

It had been daylight savings time for a week. The sky was still largely blue with little white remains of clouds. But it was getting darker by the minute, as if someone were slightly turning down a dimmer switch. The street was empty. A block away I could make out the bass of the jukebox. Inside there were seven or eight people — mostly sitting at the bar.

Barb, on a high stool, was alone at a table by the window. Her head jerked toward the door as I entered and her eyes flashed. I looked around casually and then fixed my gaze on her, as if surprised. I smiled innocently.

I passed the u-shaped bar just as the juke box was changing songs.

"Well, hello," I said grabbing a stool and sitting across from her. "Isn't this cozy?" "Twist and Shout" started playing on the juke box.

"What do you want?" she glowered at me, her face reflecting

the red of a beer sign on the opposite wall.

"Oh nothing," I replied. "I was just out for a stroll and thought I might stop by for a coke."

She looked at me and then at her watch. She couldn't ask me to leave and yet she had to get rid of me.

"I'm going to tell Mom. You're not even eighteen," Barb threatened.

"Go ahead," I countered, knowing she wouldn't.

"Want something to drink?" I asked as I scooted over to the bar and caught the attention of the young bartender. He wore a tight Pabst Blue Ribbon t-shirt. It was 7:40."

"One of the baseball teams on the TV scored a run. The guys watching let out what seemed to me to be a somewhat forced cheer.

It was at that moment Harry poked his head through the door. What Barb didn't know was that I had written him a note too. Oh, not an anonymous one, but a message from me on plain paper saying that he and I needed to talk. "Meet me at Heather's at 7:45 tonight, but if by some fluke Barb should suspect I am meeting you and show up, duck back out immediately or there'll be a scene. I have to talk to you about her.

- signed Dora."

Barb gasped. I started to count peanut shells on the floor.

She got up. "I've got to go to the john," she said lamely, meaning to head for the front door which was by the washrooms, and call after him.

"I do too," I said nonchalantly, "I'll go with you."

That's when she sunk down. I think she realized this was hopeless. Harry was gone.

We walked home together ten minutes later. Neither spoke. Then after we were in bed for the night, with the lights off, she suddenly broke the silence.

"I don't know what to do Dora."

"What do you mean?"

"Harry's been coming on to me and now he's really acting weird."

"Harry?" I said innocently.

"I know. I know. You thought he had a thing for you, and I'm sorry but..."

"But what?"

"When you hear what I have to say, you might actually be grateful."

I could barely contain myself. I had poisoned her mind against that betraying bastard and now...now she was turning to me for help. And help is exactly what she would get.

I had seen these women in the bar with their heavy arms, dark eyebrows and bleached blond hair. Smoking, drinking shots and beer, dressed in tank tops and full skirts to cover their big hips and fat butts. Chatting it up with the guys in baseball caps. That's what awaited us if we stayed here in Rockdale. That was our future, or lack of it. What difference did it make if you were smart or creative or worked hard. You were only as good as the guys who settled for you at the end of the night.

"He wants money. He wants sex. His demands are more and more crazy. I want to go to college not get stuck pregnant by some guy," Barb was crying softly now. "But I can't trust myself either. Oh I just don't know what the hell to do."

"We'll figure something out. Now there are the two of us, not just you anymore."

"You couldn't know it, but Harry was suppose to meet me tonight. That's why I was over at Heather's."

"But you didn't. I mean, he showed up. I saw him. Then he ducked out again.

"It was seeing you there with me too."

"Maybe, but I do know what you should do"

"What?"

I went over and sat on the end of her bed. I said, "The next time he sends you a note we're both going to meet him. Together."

"Thanks, Dora."

"Now no more crying. Go to sleep."

The next time he sent her a note, I thought. Out the window a ripple of clouds paraded across the distant full moon. I not only knew when his next note was coming, but where it would say to meet. That place where all this began. And late at night. With or without a moon.

Day Three – Meaning

Jack Lehman

What I would recommend to you, what I did myself with my first novella, is to find something you really like and imitate it chapter by chapter. Have corresponding characters and scenes that eventually arc dramatically. When I wrote *Man with One Ear* I would read a chapter of *Treasure Island*, go for a bike ride and think about what I was going to do and a few days later draft something up. Then I would read the next chapter and repeat the process. *Treasure Island* was about a crew on a ship, mine was about a film crew making and independent film. Jim Hawkins became Max Jordan, and the one-legged pirate, Long John Silver, morphed into the one-eared Steven Livengood, a con-man/father figure.

Some of the best known novellas are: John W. Campbell's *Who Goes There?*, John Steinbeck's *Of Mice and Men*, George Orwell's *Animal Farm*, Anthony Burgess's *A Clockwork Orange*, Isaac Asimov's *Nightfall*, Herman Melville's *Billy Budd, Sailor*, Truman Capote's *Breakfast at Tiffany's*, Ernest Hemingway's *The Old Man and the Sea*, Robert Louis Stevenson's *The Strange Case of Dr Jekyll and Mr Hyde*, Charles Dickens' *A Christmas Carol*, H.G. Wells' *The Time Machine*, Philip Roth's *Goodbye, Columbus*, Joseph Conrad's *Heart of Darkness*, Thornton Wilder's *The Bridge of San Luis Rey*, Jack Kerouac's *The Subterraneans*, Thomas Pynchon's *The Crying of Lot 49* and Stephen King's *Rita Hayworth and Shawshank Redemption*.

The approach I'm recommending allows you to experience

and employ a dramatic structure that has taken someone years to learn. Meanwhile, you are gaining control by fictionalizing elements of your own life, instead of being a victim. And that, my friends, is what art provides. What makes something seem right is that its parts fit together (in a way we always want but that never happens in real life—that's why people pay you for it). But there is even more.

As individuals we don't take certain risks, but these are the things that define our emotional boundaries. In a book or play or movie we are free to let go, to be all we can be and feel all we are capable of *without* assuming the responsibilities as we have to in real life. After all, it's only a book, only a play, only a movie.

But play acting also needs to be credible. As writers we use elements our experience provides, and as audience we are leaving with something more than relief. We are gaining what others have encountered or that we could have had under different circumstances. With classics these deepen at each reading and match the perspective we need now. They speak to us; they listen to us.

Returning to *Geography*, Max has suffered a failure and now is trying to regroup with the help of another, Kim Kong. We don't find out any more about either of them. At least not directly. But through examples of Barb, Dora and Harry—in the manuscript they are examining together—we understand the complexities and pitfalls of relationships. And through that the reader can see these relationships as metaphors for his or her own. That is the ultimate compliment we can make as writers, turning readers into artists.

Think of the books we treasure most, aren't they the ones that got us thinking about their meaning *for us*, discussing our conclusions with others, going back and reading them again and again and again and each time finding something new, not because the book has changed, but because we have grown.

Notice we don't know if the manuscript account is literally true—that depends upon which of the sisters wrote it. But we have opinions based on our own needs and turn the page to find out whether or not we are right. What we have learned is that meaning is relative (that's the message that can't be denied no matter how things are resolved).

Let me take a moment and discuss point of view. In the manuscript, it seems the narrator is Flora/Dora. We see what she sees, and don't see what she doesn't. We also have her thoughts and not Barb's. Right away she becomes our representative. But what of Max and Kim. It turns out we don't have either of their thoughts. That allows the writer to slip some things past the reader which can be revealed at an appropriate time later.

Point of view is a mechanism for you to present and withhold information. It keeps suspense and the reader turning the page. That is also true for the writer caught in the creative process. He or she creates characters (or uses aspects of people the writer knows), but there are also the dynamics of those characters taking on a life of their own. And we, as writers, have to turn the page to find out where they are leading us. So "control" is somewhat misleading. It means we can relive something on our terms (we are choosing the scenes to use and those we are not going to use) but the people in those scenes may surprise us. And sometimes the scenes do to. What we thought would be a strong one, flounders; and what may have started as a necessary transition scene, jumps off the page. My suggestion, write the scenes without worrying about their order and in the second draft switch them around into an arc that grabs the reader, then complicates the plot, reaches a turning point (after which nothing will ever be the same) and finishes up with a short resolution that ties up the loose ends.

To be honest when I wrote *Geography* I had no idea where it was going. I just wanted to back myself into a corner and then get out. There is foreshadowing in the form of Harry's obituary, so we know something happened to him and of course the women leaving town soon afterward is suspicious. But more important than foreshadowing is what Andre Dubus calls "after shadowing." This means things the reader passes over, but in the end when looking back point to the climax. I think that is what leads to our feeling of completeness. Things that didn't seem to fit together, do.

Let me finish with a few words about the novella. It has gone in and out of fashion, mostly, I think, because of printing constraints. It is expensive to publish a traditional book so those who do, favor hefty cover prices which require a large number of pages for the price. Short stories were once popular magazine fare but in this age of *People* the norm seems to favor photos of celebrities buying groceries. On the other hand Kindle, Nook, iPads are offering much more convenient reads at low cost because there isn't the printing, storing and distributing. I think people will buy, not long novels, but novellas. Their time has arrived. And yours has too.

Jack Lehman

Night Five – A Strange Claim

Jack Lehman

Chapter 5

A Strange Claim

When I next phoned Kim on Thursday she seemed distant. At first I thought it was because I caught her at an inconvenient time. But with the second call I began to wonder if it weren't something else.

I knew she had enjoyed our reading the manuscript together at the coffee shop. She had been animated in her talk about it on the drive back to her place. Was there something in the story that later gave her reason to be concerned? In my now-plentiful spare time I came up with three possibilities.

First, she may have thought I was using this as a way to get closer to her. True, there was enough account executive in me to be capable of using something, anything, to manipulate another person. But she didn't know that.

Second, it appeared there might be some hidden aggressiveness, even violence in my family, and perhaps in me. I did know that Harry was dead and probably he'd been murdered. And here in *Swimming by the Cemetery* the narrator was plotting something against the person in the story with Harry's same name. Even the title seemed foreboding. Of course it might well be a fictional account of something real that had happened years earlier. But again, who could blame Kim for being suspicious.

The final possibility I felt was even more troublesome than the first two, believe it or not. It was the words written by Flora, or "Dora" as the narrator calls herself, about the women in the bar. Was Kim thinking that she too was settling for something in her relationship with me? Here I was thirty-six, alone, unemployed and full of self-doubt. Charlie Nash had said it. I was "a disappointment," and now Kim who herself had known difficulty may be wondering if she didn't deserve better.

Almost as if in answer to that last thought, the phone rang. It was a call from Aunt Babe's attorney, Zachery.

"Well the estate sale went well," he began. "Fine turnout. What wasn't sold was purchased by a resale shop."

"Good, good," I answered.

"The same shop is going to drop off the oriental carpet you wanted."

"That's great. I'd forgotten about it. I'm not sure where to put it but they can leave it in the apartment storage area in the basement."

When I relayed the news in the second call to Kim (who seemed distant), I added that he had said there was some unexpected news…a possible complication, though there might not be anything to it.

"Oh, what's that?" she asked, suddenly seeming interested again.

"My aunt's lawyer said to me that he received a phone call early this morning from Rockdale, Wisconsin."

"Rockdale, where your parents were from?"

"Yes, well the call was from a man who made a rather strange claim."

"What do you mean?"

"He said that he had just read about my aunt's death…"

"Yes, yes, spit it out…"

"He had just heard of her death and he said that he, not I, was the rightful heir to her estate."

Kim was dumbfounded. "That's impossible, isn't it?" she stammered.

"That's what I told him. Neither of my aunts had children and I'm an only child. The Rockdale man says he was put up for adoption before he was even born, and only this year discovered who his birth mother was."

"What's his name?" she asked.

"Zachery said he didn't have the man's name with him, he was calling from a cell phone in the car. But he did remember that the first name was Harry."

"Harry!" Kim exclaimed.

I told Kim, "The lawyer thought the last name was "Broderick" but that was probably the family name of his adopting parents. He wasn't positive about that."

"About 'Broderick' or that it was the last name of the people who adopting him?" Kim asked.

"About either, really. But listen, Zachery said his associate was looking into it. He told me not to worry; it might be some crank. He said they get that all the time. Someone sees an obituary and if there may be money involved and no offspring, they think they can grab a piece of it."

"But what about your aunt's will?"

"Well that's curious too," I replied. "It says 'next of kin' but doesn't identify me by name. Sometimes people do that. They don't know when they are going to die so want to keep it open in case circumstances change."

Kim thought for a minute and then asked, "But hadn't this attorney just been with her in the hospital. Didn't she know she was dying? In fact why else would she have him visit her there? We have to get back into that manuscript."

Kim said she would meet, and that dinner at my place this Saturday would be fine.

There was a severe thunderstorm that night. Rain beat on the roof of my third-floor apartment. I watched it stream across my bedroom window. Lightning flashes were like flashbulbs on those old cameras and in my dream I saw things both as negatives and positives. Oddly I didn't dream about my present situation but about the rainy season in Vietnam. We had been sent there to set up a field hospital in advance of a buildup of American troops.

Though I was a lieutenant I worked side by side other junior officers and sergeants with machetes clearing the ground for tents and a helicopter landing area. Later, after the facility and all its equipment were in place we realized how futile this had been. When the time came casualties were evacuated by the copters directly from the front lines to the brick and mortar hospital in Saigon.

But here's what I dreamed. It was when we were still back at Fort Riley, Kansas, being briefed. A sergeant, Billy Jars, stood up and said he'd rather go to hell than be sent to Vietnam. Two weeks later he was struck by lightning while out fishing on a boat at night. I heard that thunder. Saw the fork of lighting leave the sky. The reflection — my reflection — standing in that boat before I fell into the water. And then I was sinking below the surface. And now in my bed I listened to the sounds of a storm all around me.

I was not a pacifist. The reality is I could never hit anything shooting a rifle on a firing range so I didn't see much sense carrying one around. Even if I aimed at a target, my glasses would steam up. But I could never have shot anyone, even if my life depended on it. Telling Kim about Vietnam would probably not be a good idea though because her father was Chinese and I don't think any country has ever appreciated American's meddling in their North/South wars.

The next day I started to clean my apartment. I washed the accumulation of dishes in the sink, hauled my laundry, including sheets and pillow cases, to the laundromat and bought some groceries after checking a simple recipe in my wife's old *New York*

Times Cookbook.

There was something about the cleaning that reminded me of Carolyn. Maybe it was the smell of Dust Off table polisher or Ajax or the sound of the Windex bottle squirting. Like my mom she was a compulsive cleaner. My childhood was filled with the sound of the vacuum cleaner, and I remember how Mom would leave it in the middle of the room when she was done, almost as a monument, in case we had missed the drone of its being shoved back and forth over the carpet. Back and forth, back and forth. Or how she would leave the step ladder up after doing the windows. My mother would never ask me to cut the grass, but haul the push mower out and start grunting until I would come out an relieve her.

Carolyn was the same. Once a year she would take everything out of the kitchen cabinets, ostensibly to wipe down the cans of soup, tomato paste, seasoning and bottles of vanilla, vinegar and olive oil. Putting them back was another matter. I came to think that men might communicate their business successes and frustrations through financial reports but women had mastered the vengeful art of using household chores to express anger.

All I had in the apartment were some pieces of furniture Carolyn had never liked. Dishes and silverware from Wal-Mart. I did have two wonderful floor lamps, some black and white posters of Paris and a queen size futon and frame I'd splurged on. That was about it. Oh, a big flat-screen TV of course and my half-way decent computer and printer. I like to think my place has a minimalist Japanese feel, but others may see it as barren and depressing. In honor of this special occasion I went out and bought some scented candles and a few quiet CD's I could play on my computer. And two good wine glasses.

The apartment itself was on the top floor and relatively quiet—at least there weren't tenants stomping around overhead. And the view of my neighborhood street from tree-top level was enchanting. No one would think they were in a forest, but, especially this time of year, in the morning, there was the shimmering, swishing of new leaves. I had no idea who my neighbors were, nor did I want to know.

That's how later in the day I came to lose myself in house cleaning. It was rather nice—having the windows thrown open, classical music playing, visions of Kim dancing in my head. I had lied to her. At the time it had seemed the simplest thing to do, but now I knew I would have to face up to the truth. Carolyn and I had not divorced. We had been separated and living apart. In fact we each had our own attorneys and were working through some kind of a settlement. That wasn't going very well, she was aware of the inheritance – that was real enough – and wanted her half as my wife.

If Kim pressed me, I would say, "Yes, there are problems. We are having difficulties about the settlement, about dividing up our marital property." But maybe something would happen to changes things. Maybe, like my mother, Carolyn would drown.

Jack Lehman

Night Six – Ghosts

Jack Lehman

Chapter 6

Ghosts

I buzzed her up. Since I had moved to this one-room apartment a year and a half ago I'd had less than three visitors by the front entrance, and one of them was the mailman requesting I sign for a registered letter.

My heart started beating as soon as I opened the door. It wasn't her short black hair and how her bangs hung a little over her eyes or even her fresh inviting smile. It was the overnight bag hanging down from her left hand. In the right she held a small bouquet of tulips which she held out to me like a little kid would.

"Come in," I said taking the flowers. "Does the suitcase mean what I think it means?"

"I'm staying the night, if that's OK," she answered.

"Oh, I have to check the reservation book," I joked.

Kim smiled even broader, if possible, and I saw the living room she entered as she must have. Pretty bare of furniture and pictures, but the flickering votive candles I had placed on the floor along two sides of the otherwise dimly lit room did throw interesting shadows on the walls. I had placed a colorful Native American blanket over the back of the convertible futon-sofa and I'd purchased a few leather floor pillows just for this occasion. I liked the varnished wood floor but imagined this is where I would put the Oriental rug from my aunt. And that would be opulent.

"Let me take your things," I said hanging her faux rabbit fur jacket in the hall closet and putting her bag in the corner.

"Sit down. Like some wine?" I asked.

"Sure," she answered but followed me into the kitchenette. I turned from the counter and took her in my arms.

"Tonight is about us," I said. "Let the manuscript go until tomorrow morning. I want…"

"I know what you want, but let's eat first. I'm starved and whatever you're cooking smells super. What is it? What's baking in the oven?"

"An old family recipe," I lied. "I have to warn you though, it's pretty exotic. Ever hear of…meatloaf?"

"Now that sounds like Wisconsin," she nodded approvingly.

We settled on the couch and I poured us each a glass of merlot. I had pushed play to start a CD of classic Miles Davis ballads on the computer right after Kim had rung the bell.

"Nice," she smiled listening to the music, sipping her glass of wine. She wore a loose silk blouse and leather pants. I noticed the heels on her boots that gave her a little extra height tonight.

"So, what would you like to talk about?" I began.

"How about you," she said with a devilish grin.

"No, you know more than enough about me already, but I

hardly know anything about you."

"I'm afraid it's not a very happy story," she said. "You sure?"

"Of course. Go ahead. I'd love to know your background."

"Well, my father was Chinese. 'Kong' is my family name. My mother isn't. He came here from Macau right after world War II. He was trained as an electrical engineer, but when he arrived in Chicago, he couldn't find a job in his profession so he worked in a new convenience store on the South Side."

"Like a 7-11?"

"Yes, but this was well before them. Just a small chain. Anyway he was a good worker and a smart business man. After awhile he owned and operated two new locations of the franchise in the Northwest suburbs. Then he got into real estate. It was about this time that he met my mother. They were married and bought a bungalow not far from here, around Clark and Peterson."

"I know that area," I said. And did I know it. "That's quite a success story. Why don't you think it is happy.?"

"Let me get to that. He went from a convenience store clerk, to selling real estate, to investing in apartment buildings and eventually condos by Lake Michigan. But here's what's sad. We never saw him. My mother was going deaf and whether it was because of him or her hearing loss she became very withdrawn. I was about ten at this time, with a brother who was five years younger. I would write notes to her and she would write notes back to me. I think that may be how I first became enamored with reading other people's writings—poems, essays, memoirs."

"Interesting."

"Then my father fell in love with a Chinese woman. She was married and had a daughter my same age. He began living a double life. Now you see why I say this is a sad story."

"Go on."

"The woman was married, as I said, but my dad bought her husband's silence through gifts, first of money then of properties he had acquired. It was a very subtle, but insidious extortion. The man became more and more demanding. My dad turned to alcohol and gambling. All that he had earned through his hard work and cleverness went down the drain."

"And you and your mother could do nothing?"

"No. My younger brother would fight with him, but that just made things worse. That brother now runs a Chinese-buffet restaurant called 'Main Moon.' He even hired my father to work for a time. By then he was an old, drunken beaten-down man. Fortunately there had been at least enough money for me to go to junior college and after I graduated I moved out, leaving all that behind."

"And you got married."

"That was a mistake. It only lasted one year. I'm afraid I was just a little too anxious to be part of a real family. My ex-husband was in the service at the time. We both knew we were unsuited for each other, and when Liviana was diagnosed as autistic, he seemed to want to get as far away from both of us as he could. At least then."

"That was seven or eight years ago?"

"Right. I started at Lawson and Abrams two years ago, and last year I met you."

I took a sheet from a post-it pad that happened to be on the little side table and wrote Kim a note. It said: "Let's eat!"

She read it and nodded. We moved to the kitchenette. Her tulips were in a vase I had placed on the small table.

Let me describe two things at once to you. For some strange reason that is how they are imbedded in my memory.

We set the plates out on the table, I took the meatloaf from the oven and placed it on a platter. I pulled out the futon, placing the folded Native American blanket to one side and grabbed sheets, a blanket and two feather pillows from the closet.

I cut the skin of each baked potato, pried the halves apart, spread butter and sour cream down the middle. I opened her blouse and stared at the whiteness of her skin. While I made up the bed she removed her boots and pants. When I was done and I turned to look at her, she slowly let the black silk top fall to the floor. She was relatively flat-chested and didn't wear a bra. I noticed the gentle buds of her breast. I took off my own clothes. She climbed into the futon bed.

The meatloaf was cooked to perfection. The bacon and barbeque sauce on it were crispy and tangy. The texture of each slice melted at the advance of a fork and the green French beans were a perfect complement to the red wine, potatoes and meat. And then there were the slices of warm cherry pie with whipped cream.

She was like a plaything in my arms. I felt I was making love for the first time, except she made it seem I knew what I was doing. Afterwards I could hear the gentle panting of both our breaths. Whatever was outside of this room just didn't seem to matter. I can't remember what we said to one another. I got up and blew the candles out. Before long we were both asleep.

And that is what should have filled my dreams, but it didn't. Instead I found myself back in Rockdale, Wisconsin. I wasn't myself, for I could tell this was years ago before I was born. And I wasn't Harry Davidson either. At least not exactly. But I was imagining things as they would have happened to him after the last chapter of my aunts' manuscript. He was looking at a note he thought came from Barb, but I knew had actually been written by her sister. He was wondering what it meant.

"Quarry" what a strange word. Once I had actually looked it up in the dictionary to make sure that I was not misinterpreting it. The primary definition is a large pit from which stone has been extracted. But another meaning is, "an animal pursued by a hunter, hound, predatory mammal or bird of prey; a thing or person that is chased or sought."

Their movie was done. It had been shown to the Creative Writing class complete with a musical accompaniment (cuts of pop music recorded on a tape recorder). Mr. Larson had been pleased. The three who produced it had even taken a bow in front of the class when the movie was over. And now I was watching Harry drive from Cambridge to Rockdale late on a blustery night. I could see him at the wheel of his van, almost like he was in an old black and white movie, headlights from passing cars briefly illuminating his tense face.

Across the bridge, up the hill on the other side, down the back dirt road. There was a gate that was never closed. He headed toward the base of the quarry as he'd been directed. The wind was blowing. There was no moon or stars. No sign of other cars. He stopped the van and shut off the engine. There was a knock at the window. No one was there.

In real life, had it been me, I would have started up the engine, turned on the headlights and headed back home, but in dreams we don't seem to have choices. And this was Harry, not me. Or so I thought. He slowly opened the door and stepped out.

"Barb," he shouted, "it's me. It's Harry."

Nothing.

"Barb," the man began again. But suddenly he was struck across the back of his head by a shovel whirling through the dark. I couldn't be sure. But the woman swinging the shovel seemed to be wearing a bandana. As he dropped to his hands and knees it came crashing down on his head again.

That's when I awoke with a start. I was relieved to find myself in my uncomfortable, but familiar futon. There beside me I could see in the dim light through the window from the streetlights below was my angel, Kim.

I thought about what I had dreamt. Perhaps it was the melancholy of her family story. Or maybe my own apprehension about how the evening would go. In any case I couldn't sleep. I lay there looking out at the night. I could hear the leaves of trees blowing. Was that how it had happened for Harry? In the story Dora had promised Barb that the two of them would face him together. Or was this just something she had said to appease her sister. Gain her trust. He had been found years later in a quarry. But maybe, maybe I was just using information I had gained recently to create this account of it in my dream.

I had just started to drift off to sleep again. I was trying to think of our lovemaking, something, anything to regain my composure. It was then in the wind that I heard the sound of water running from a faucet. A ratchety sound but clear and distinct. A tub. Water spilling over the side.

Day Four – Lunch

Jack Lehman

These last two chapters provide back-story on both Max and Kim that complicate the plot.

Max relivesan unhappy life with his wife and his mother's suicide which seems to substantiate his premonition that the sisters killed Harry. And Kim….

From Kim's part we see that she has every reason to distrust men. What is intriguing to me is that I commandeered her background from that of Lorine Niedecker, a poet born over 200 years ago who lived about twenty miles from where I do now. When I first heard about Niedecker's father, I couldn't imagine how his daughter felt, especially since his mistress had a daughter about her same age. It is tempting to apply a little literary psychotherapy to the poet's work based on this, but perhaps that wouldn't be accurate. I did the next best thing using it as my fictional character's imprint.

Both Max and Kim are locked into things from their past and the climax, I know, will somehow be when one or the other or bothof them break free of the past. How? I didn't really know when I wrote this part, the reader and I would both have to wait and see.

There is another useful element at work, in Max's dreaming. We don't know if they are true or not but they flesh out the murder scene in the quarry and raise a question. Emotionally, is there a difference between what happens and what we think happens?

You wake up from an unfavorable dream about your wife and she says, "What's the matter with you?" "Nothing," you reply, "just a bad dream." But you are angry just like when watching a suspenseful movie, you actually become afraid or seeing a musical comedy you might feel elated. The feelings are genuine, even if their subject matter isn't.

What power this gives the writer and reader is the ability to deal with real feelings through the use of fiction. Even off the page we all have the ability to project a happy or an unhappy life by convincing ourselves it is so.

A third element of these chapters is the alternating between food and sex. It makes something that might be hard to portray, vivid, by comparing it to something easy to portray that we have all experienced and enjoyed.

One thing stands for another. Opening a baked potato is a way of portraying undressing Kim, their examination of the aunts' manuscript is symbolic of me and you examining *Geography of Sleep* in terms of our lives.

Science may deal with the physical world but literature, through the use of metaphor, is able to examine love, death, fear, happiness (all of which are hard to quantify) in terms of comparisons to accessible experiences in our day-by-day lives. And is the result any less true than those emotions generated in dreams?

I had a little fantasy about the real life Kim who I saw in a business capacity, was perplexed by Niedecker's family environment, and maybe, just maybe, wonder if my mother had any secrets she didn't share with me. What do these things mean and how did I feel about them? Time to find out.

Jack Lehman

Night Seven –

Hermitage

Chapter 7

Hermitage

Before going to sleep that night, but after our making love, Kim had said that she regretted cutting herself off from her mother and talking about her had made her realize that she wanted to visit her. She lived in the same bungalow where Kim had been raised as a child.

"I want to go with you," I said.

"What? Why? I appreciate your interest but this is between her and me."

"I understand," I replied, "It's just that sometimes it is easier to do these things if you are not alone. Besides…Well, this seems like a strange coincidence, but I grew up in that same Rogers Park neighborhood."

"What? I don't believe it. I never saw you there. The first time I met you was at work."

"Remember, I'm twenty years older than you, and I don't know where you lived exactly. I was over on Hood Ave."

"We lived on Hermitage," she said, "5923 to be exact. But why would you want to go with me to visit my mom? She's old and deaf. It's not like there will be pleasant reminiscences and tea."

"I want to. That's all." I couldn't tell her the real reason. Her story had opened up part of my own. Perhaps that was why I had dreamed what I had. After I had gone away to grad school, my own relationship with my mother had troubled me then and it troubled me today. What I wanted to do was to go back and face a part of my past too. My father had since died and this was a way to return, not to the exact place I remembered, but to a similar one. The fact that Kim's mother wouldn't speak was a benefit. The fact that I could do this with someone else, a real gift.

"Well, OK, if you're sure," she finally agreed.

"Let's go tomorrow."

"Tomorrow?"

But before she could object any further I rolled over on top of her and we began another romp in the hay.

There was a cassette I heard a few years ago by an editor of *Psychology Today* in which he suggested an interesting exercise. He told listeners to stop the program and, on a sheet of paper, draw a diagram of the house where they lived when they were between eight and ten. I did this as I was listening to it, detailing each floor.

Two things surprised me. First, I knew I could never do such accurate diagrams of the two or three places I had lived in as an adult. Second, I not only remembered to juxtaposition of the rooms to one another but also things only an eight-year-old would know—the crawl space under the back porch accessible only through a basement window, a hideout beneath the attic stairs, the area between the wood panel and stone wall of the cellar, backs of closets where I hid during games of hide and seek.

I was driving in the car when I heard this exercise and actually pulled over into a MacDonald's parking lot to do it on paper. It was like a map, a treasure map, to an old world that I had thought I'd forgotten, and each room, each space, seemed to have an emotion connected to it. For example, I remembered the couch with wrought iron legs in the breakfast room off of the kitchen. It was in front of a flush radiator and there I would lay watching my mother in the kitchen prepare spaghetti for our family meal. My dad came home by train each night at 5:10; we would eat at 6. I could smell the tomato sauce, hear her humming, know that gentle snowflakes were falling in the window above the radiator that looked out on our backyard with its single cherry tree. The bark on that tree's branches was dark as red wine and smooth. On the top of each branch was a frosting of new snow.

The garage. My God, remember how those old wooden doors (before the ones that rolled up over the car) were always rotting along the bottom, dragged across the stones of the alley because of lose hinges that made the doors sag. The ladders hung on brackets outside along one of the garage walls. The clutter that never went away piled in one of the inside corners.

"Hi, Mom," Kim said with an exaggeration so her mother could read her lips. She knew we were coming. There was a service you could call and volunteers would take your message, type it out and somehow send it to some kind of monitor of the deaf person. The mother had typed back her excitement which the woman on the phone then read to Kim matter of factly.

As we drove over, I could tell Kim was nervous. It had been several years. Birthday and holiday cards had been exchanged (including some flowery letters and little gifts to Liviana).

I asked Kim how she felt.

"Like I'm going to visit the dead," she replied.

There was parking on the street a few houses down. The sidewalks, the front yards, everything seemed small, close together —all the big elm trees had died off Kim told me. These bungalows with their brick fronts, cement stoops and windows with gauze-like curtains and shades half drawn, were exactly like the one in which I grew up.

Kim took her hand from mine as if we were eight years old entering the world of adults who might disapprove.

Her mother hugged Kim and ignored my outstretched hand. She attempted to say something to us but I couldn't make out what it was. Tenderly Kim put her arm around her mom's shoulder and guided her through the front hallway, into the living room. I followed.

After we were seated and the two women silently sipped some tea the older woman had poured, I made a feeble excuse to use the bathroom. Once behind the mother I said to Kim in a very soft voice, "I also want to take a quick look around, OK?"

Because of her deafness, the mother had not heard me. Kim

looked at me. She seemed peeved, but with her mom staring at her, she felt unable to say anything. The mom had a small pad of paper and she and her daughter were now exchanging notes once again.

As I walked back through the dining room, past a doorway into a hall of four or five doors and then into the kitchen, I had the weirdest feeling that I was shrinking in size. This was almost the exact layout of my parent's old house. Probably all the houses on the block, and in neighboring blocks shared similar floor plans. The kitchen and then the breakfast room. It was only when I returned to this interior hallway of doorways that I noticed something strange. The first door I opened was the master bedroom. The bed and dresser looked shabby but were more or less what I would have expected. But the second door led to an empty bedroom as did the third. Empty except for some packing boxes. Kim's mother was packing up to leave. The fourth, fifth and sixth doors were to the attic, the bathroom and the basement respectively. I didn't have time to explore other floors. I went into the bathroom, shut the door and washed my hands in the old-fashioned sink. Before leaving I reached over and flushed the toilet, then realized that Kim's mother wouldn't hear this anyway.

The two of them were still seated around the coffee table as I had left them. Kim looked up. Then her mother.

In that moment I saw that there was absolutely no recognition in the mother's expression. She did not remember me. I was a stranger appearing from the back of her house. But it was more than that. She jumped to her feet and began spewing, what I recognized as Chinese. She leaped at me like some kind of old lioness ready to scratch my eyes out.

I backed into the wall. There was actually saliva running from her mouth as she spit words at me I didn't understand.

Her arms swung wildly at my head. Kim was trying to grab her from behind, but the older woman was quite a bit larger than her daughter and there was a vehemence about her that was not easily subdued. I slid along the wall to the dining-room entrance. As soon as I was beyond her grasp, she suddenly stopped. Her eyes closed, she started to turn in a circle.

Kim stepped back.

The mother twirled faster and faster until her knee gave way and she went crashing to her side, into the coffee table. The hysterical woman had passed out.

"Help me get her up on the couch," Kim pleaded.

We each grabbed the mother's arms and dragged her over to the couch and then slid her up to the seat. She was still unconscious and when we let go, she slumped into the back of the couch.

"Will she be OK?" I stammered.

"I think so." Kim replied.

I remembered that she had had some experience with Liviana's seizures. I didn't know what to do.

"Why don't you wait outside in the car," Kim suggested. "I think the shock of seeing me and then her confused mental condition brought this on. Let's make it as simple as possible for her when she wakes up. I don't want to leave her. In fact why don't you drive off somewhere to a bookstore or coffee shop and come back in about an hour. Honk, and if everything is all right I'll just come out."

"Sure," I said, "whatever you think."

But I took one last glance at the unconscious woman. She had white hair. Her eyes were closed and her mouth hung open, but I could tell she had a determined jaw. She was dressed in a house coat such as my Aunt Flora used to wear around the house. Kim was kneeling in front of her mom. The two looked nothing alike.

"What was she yelling at me?" I asked, knowing Kim spoke Chinese.

"It doesn't matter. She thought you were my ex-husband, that's all. Now please go, before she wakes up."

"But I want to know."

"Later."

"No, now. You owe that much to me."

Kim she sighed and reluctantly told me what her mother had said.

I got into the car. This was not a neighborhood of stores or coffeehouses. I knew I could drive over to Clark Street, a few blocks away and find some place to kill an hour, but for some reason I didn't want to. Instead I turned right on Paullina and headed over to my old address on Hood.

I slowly drove past the house where I grew up and pulled into the curb where there was a space because of the fire hydrant. It looked pretty much the same. Things didn't change much. I remembered an old joke about Chicago. It went: A bunch of people in New York said, "Gee, I'm enjoying the crime and the poverty, but it just isn't cold enough. Let's go west." And that supposedly how Chicago got started.

I turned off the engine and checked the clock. It was 2 PM. I'd wait here until 3. Seeing Kim with her mother, made me think of what things must have been like when she was Liviana's age. What my life was like when I was eight and living at home. There was a tension between my two aunts ten blocks away, but there was also tension in my house between my mother and father. I could always feel it. Not until I visited my friends homes and ate meals with their families did I realize this was not something everyone experienced. I would ask my mother and she would say it was nothing or I was imagining things. Now today, Kim's mother had yelled at me. She had said in Chinese, "You can't come back here. You can't." She thought I was her drunken son-in-law. I wasn't, but the words still resonated. "You can't come back."

"Oh," I told myself sitting in that car parked near my old home, "Oh yes I can!"

After an hour I returned to the mother's house and waited. I went up the front stairs and rang the bell. There was no answer. I tried the door. It was locked. Kim was nowhere in sight.

Night Eight – Possibilities

Jack Lehman

Chapter 8

Possibilities

After I got back into my car, I realized what to do. I pulled out my cell phone, checked to see if I'd missed any messages (I hadn't) and phoned Kim. There was only her voice mail. I left this message: "Hi, Kim, it's me Max. Say I'm back at your mom's house and it doesn't appear she or you are here. What's going on? Are you all right? Give me a call on my cell."

And she did. Almost immediately, before I had driven all the way back home.

"Max. I'm so sorry. We're at the Edgewater Hospital. I couldn't get Mom to snap out of her faint so I called an ambulance and they brought us here. I just didn't have time to call."

"How's she doing?"

"She's OK. They did something to bring her around and now she's resting. I'm just trying to catch my breath."

"Do you want me to come there?"

"No. God, no. It was just the stress of her seeing me and not recognizing who you were."

"What about you? How do you feel?" I asked.

"Me. Oh, I'm alright," she sounded as if she were distancing herself from me. "Listen, I've got to go."

"But how will you get home? What about Liviana?"

"I called my Ex who has her this weekend and they are swinging by to pick me up. I'll call you," and as if she wanted to be clear that she didn't mean right away, she added, "...early next week. Wednesday. I'll telephone you Wednesday."

"Kim..." I started to reply, but she had already hung up.

Well that was a simple enough explanation of her disappearance, I thought as I pulled around back of my building and started up the wood stairs. Perhaps that was my trouble in terms of my relationship with my aunts. I was looking for something complex and there was a more direct, more simple explanation.

I opened the door and turned on the kitchen light. It was 5:35 pm. the dishes from last night's dinner were still in the sink. Maybe I was imagining it, but there also seemed to be a slight whiff of our sex in the air.

I went over to my briefcase and took the manuscript out. I turned on the floor lamp in the other room and flopped down on the futon couch.

Swimming by the Cemetery shown as enigmatically as ever from the front cover. I wanted to think, perhaps more objectively, about the opening chapters. Holding the papers across my chest, I closed my eyes and thought how someone might conclude there were three possibilities.

First, both aunts had written this as they may have co-written other novels. That's what it said on the title-page after all. Why not take this at face value? But it just didn't sound like the two women I had described to Kim. Wouldn't writing for them be more like playing a game of chess against one another? One aunt would write something that created a conflict between characters that was almost like an attack on her co-author's sensibilities, then that woman would twist the action around to do the same. There would be tension, mirroring the anger between the two women.

If real collaboration were the case, it almost had to be against Harry who was found dead: two high school misfits, years later, trying to create the impression they had both achieved something from a school experience. That I could see them cooperating on. They had taken the murder of this young boy and years later capitalized on it for their own purposes. It even employed their imagined connection with a high-school jock, and would explain why my dying Aunt Babe had wanted me to read this. It had less to do with the relationship of the two woman and more that their nephew would remember them both as somehow special. What this left unresolved was the animosity between the two women I had witnessed. And what about Harry Broderick and the haunting image of Flora swinging a shovel like a weapon?

A second possibility could be that this account was not fiction. That it was a confession given to Aunt Babe by Flora and now was being passed on to me. This choice offered a "simple explanation." In that case someone like Kim would realize some of the incidents in the story could be verified…in old yearbooks, by Rockdale newspapers articles of the time, maybe even through talking to Harry Broderick. Why wouldn't I call "Information," get his number, confront him by phone? The names of the two on the cover was perplexing, but maybe there was an explanation for that too.

Aunt Flora had never married. Perhaps she was a Lesbian who distrusted all men. Whatever had happened to her, this betrayal or what it had led to, could be the reason. Even her being attracted to teaching might be traced to some adolescent experience she had had with school.

If that were the case what about Babe? Why would she have kept this to herself? Perhaps she had to because she was married to a policeman. But if she were angry enough, even if she had only understood it by getting the manuscript years later, wouldn't she have opted to see Flora punished?

A third possibility was the most insidious and, in some way, also the most credible. What if Aunt Flora had nothing to do with the manuscript? What if it was something Babe had devised after her sister died to make herself look good? If that were the case this could possibly be pure fiction. Maybe there was or was not a Harry. It wouldn't matter. I tried to think about Aunt Babe. She was a big, loud woman, who did things in a big way. Not like Flora, or like my mother. My mother. Why was she missing from all this?

I had gone into the Army after college and after a year or two of indecision after my discharge, I attended graduate school at the University of Michigan under the GI Bill. I was studying curriculum development in their Masters program besides earning a teaching certificate. One of my instructors was receiving an honor out of town, I remember, so his classes had been cancelled. I had to work on a rather involved paper for another class that required reading I hadn't done. I decided I could do it at school or take the Greyhound to Chicago and the subway home for a surprise three-day work getaway.

Ordinarily I would have called but I didn't want my parents to make any fuss. I had work to be done more suited to my old bedroom than to a noisy dorm or tedious library where I already seemed to be spending too many of my days.

I entered through the back of our house and remember thinking at first no one was there. It was mid afternoon on a Friday. My dad would still be at work and my mom, doing something for the sodality at church or perhaps preparing the garden for the summer. It was the last week in April.

Setting my overnight bag full of books down in the kitchen, I called out asking if anyone were home.

There was no reply.

I walked through the house as I had just done at Kim's mother's. Every thing was in its familiar place. Then I heard it, water running in the bathroom. I knocked.

"Mom," I said, "are you in there?"

I pushed open the unlocked bathroom door and there she was in the tub on the opposite side of the room. Though her body was submerged I could tell she was naked. Water was running over the side of the tub onto the floor. Her mouth, open and half submerged, was like a small cave of water. And the water. On the floor it was bloody. In the tub, as I reached in to turn off the faucets, I could see what looked like puffs of red smoke rising from slits in her wrists.

That discovery of my mother's suicide would have been the biggest shock of my life. But that honor was reserved for my next meeting with Kim.

Day Five – We Are Story

Jack Lehman

This is when *Geography of Sleep* becomes macabre. I mention an exercise Max listened to on the car radio about drawing the house he lived in when he was eight. I not only did this but Kim's mother (shouting, "You can't go back.") is living in it. And yes, you can go back.

Oliver Sacks once said, "If we want to know about a person, we ask, 'What is her story?' 'What is his story?' For each of us *is* a story. Each of us is a biography, a singular narrative that is constructed and reconstructed continually through our senses, our actions and our words. Biologically, psychologically we're not much different from one another. To be individuals each of us must possess our own story—recollect (re-collect) our lives and act out their drama." (Oliver Sacks, *The Man Who Mistook His Wife for a Hat*)

This chapter (7) of dramatic scenes contrasts with the next (8) in which the narrator is talking directly to the reader. Max is the reader's stand in. He summarizes the situation from your standpoint. "There are three possibilities," he tells us. Whenever anyone says this, answer, "No, there are four." But why would we say that, why should we. We trust Max. He is our eyes and ears. We sympathize with his being fired, with his attraction to Kim, with his trying to come to terms with a dysfunctional family. And he has his aunts' manuscript. Right? But to quote Sacks again, "'What is his story?'"

As related to your writing, these two chapters present very different approaches. The first uses scenes—these take place at a specific time and place and employ two or more characters, each with his or her own objective for the scene, emotion and action. Kim is hesitant about re-connecting with her mother, but Max wants her to do it (in place of his revisiting his past? Which, perhaps, he feels he must do, but is hesitant). He encourages Kim to make amends with her mom and in the next chapter we think we know why—he can't with his own mother.

And there's compelling scene in which Kim's mother is trying to kill Max. She is physically struggling with him and yelling something in Chinese. Kim, using all her resources, just wants to get him out of the house. This is one of the best uses of scenes. It comes to life in the reader's theater of the imagination as opposed to the long narrative summary of the following chapter that proves a good transition but, if we close our eyes, we don't see him at a particular location. It is intellectual rather than experiential.

This ability to create dramatic scenes is something editors and publishers notice.

Most new writers use 80% narrative summary, they should use 80% scenes. Scenes create tension. Make us wonder what will happen next. Make us turn the page. Narrative summary is like a friend telling you second-hand about a move that he saw, telling you what to think. A novella needs to do both, but the emphasis—what hooks us, shows who the characters really are, complicates the plot, peaks to a climax (where everything explodes), and many of the steps in between—need to be scenes.

When I wrote the scene between Max and Kim's angry mother, I had no idea where that was going. It just seemed to be a good scene. But it leads to Max perusing his old neighborhood and his feelings about his own mother. Plus, it is a breaking point between Max and Kim (boy loses girl). At the time, it didn't seem to be a significant scene. In retrospect, it proves crucial.

I believe the most important parts of a novella are the opening scene, that hooks the reader, and the climax, which is at the top of the arc. Everything in between (whether in the present or flashback to the past) is building to that climax. My suggestion to writers is 1) have a story idea, or dilemma, you can express in one sentence, 2) figure what treatment this would best be expressed in (novel, short story, poem, personal essay, novella) and then 3) identify who your audience is. A little research (4) at a book store or library will tell show you some similar books for similar readers. You want to find out what you offer that they don't—this is key for publishers. And finally 5) set a timeline for yourself—a few chapters a week, a rough draft by Christmas, etc. Tape that to your computer screen and begin.

Jack Lehman

Night Nine –Underground Man

Jack Lehman

Chapter 9

Underground Man

There's a story by the detective-story writer, Ross Macdonald, of a middle-aged man, Stanley, who is murdered. What no one can figure out is why he seems to have been digging his own grave. Later it's discovered that his father—who had been missing for twenty years—is buried there. The father's murderer kills the son who is obsessed by this absent father and is now convinced the man is interred there. He is digging him up, somehow drawn to this "underground man." In fact, one of the characters earlier concludes that Stanley is actuality searching for himself. And we, the readers, know it is also true of the detective, Lew Archer, and probably of the author too.

This crossed my mind as I was sitting across from Kim in the booth of a micro-brewery next to the Zen Gallery, where months ago we had gone on our first date. This afternoon we had walked past the barroom and gone into a dining space to the right. Here there were old fashioned tables and solid wooden chairs. Along the far brick-wall, a half dozen raised booths. We'd taken one in the middle. Kim removed her outer sweater and we discovered we were wearing the same color turquoise shirts. Hers, a sleeveless top; mine, a make-do undershirt. The world somehow seemed less lost.

Kim asked me how I'd become a writer.

This is what I told her:

"When I was sixteen I was caught between the clutches of my two aunts who, as I told you, hated each other. The one, Flora, looked like some old photos I have seen of Gertrude Stein, her stern face glaring at the photographer, her eyes shaded by a large brim hat. The other, Aunt Babe, did not have those angular lines, and her fire was within. In fact, if you took a compass and drew a circle, then plopped two dots in it for eyes, you'd pretty much have a portrait of this tall, 350 pound woman. We like fat people because they're jolly, right? Not my aunt. She was married to a tough Irish cop, who was terrified of her. Now twenty years later I find myself looking for something. A key as to why things were the way they were.

"'Doesn't it make you wonder?' Aunt Flora, would ask me when I occasionally found myself on her overstuffed couch with its white shroud (meant to protect the fabric underneath for special occasions that never seemed to come). 'Here she is, supposedly happily married, yet getting bigger and bigger every day.' Aunt Flora had never married. Almost 40 years earlier when Flora, Babe, my mother and my grandmother had moved to Chicago from that small village in Wisconsin, my grandmother had bought this huge, three-story house where the four of them lived while the sisters attended college or trade school. When the other two sisters eventually married and their mother died, Flora remained. In fact, over time, she took in another woman as a border. Aunt Babe and her new husband bought a more modest bungalow right across the street from them.

"'She has nothing besides her teaching job and that musty old house,' Babe would confide in me over pie on Sunday afternoons when I would bike over. 'What a waste.' She'd close her eyes and shake her head as I'd watch her massive neck sway from side to side and swallow another bite of lemon meringue pie. 'And that renter of hers gives me the creeps.'"

We both ordered the tomato and mushroom bisque. Kim passed on something to drink. I got a 12oz glass of the Emerald Isle Stout.

I continued, "This was before the days when television became widespread, so each night of the summer, Aunt Flora would walk across the street to sit on the screened in front porch with Dan and Babe. After dark, as neighbors walked by on the sidewalk near the streetlamp, the two women would call their 'hellos,' then lose themselves in the latest gossip about this person. It made for interesting conversation for both were excellent story tellers. In fact, as I told you, the two sisters were writers and had collaborated on some unpublished mysteries. That's why they interested me. I dreamed someday of being an author myself.

"And my Uncle Dan was a valuable resource for their murderous tales. He could fill them in on police procedures and—these were the days of the original Richard Dailey as mayor—on some of the behind the scenes politics that made the city work. Once Dan took me to the police station where he was assigned and showed me around. He placed me in a cell and shut the door. It was just to give me the feel of prison, but it scares me to this day. That clanging sound, no chance of communicating with others, being trapped not only within a prison cell, but within yourself.

"Babe and Dan had no children. They would spoil me with food and treats. The problem was that they didn't know what youngsters liked so I'd be showered with huge quantities of things I didn't want. For example, Babe's lemon meringue pie was unusually tart to the taste, but what can you say to a woman who bakes a whole pie just for you when she knows you are coming to visit. I told my mother about the pie, but for some reason she was perfectly satisfied keeping her distance from both of her sisters and was a little miffed that her only child would bother with them himself. That was curious too.

"Once when I was small and my parents had to both be out of town I stayed with Babe and Dan over the weekend. In the top drawer of their dresser, when they thought I was taking a nap, I found my uncle's police revolver.

"Flora would write the background description of their novels. *"It was a rainy Saturday in April, small green buds, like caterpillars, had just started to appear on the bare, outstretched limbs of the giant elm trees. A 1949 Packard slowly drove down the backstreet, its tires disturbing the mirror-like puddles of water stretching from the curb on one side of the street to the other. It was a pretentious sedan. The kind a short man might drive to impress onlookers...."*

"Uncle Dan drove a Packard. He said he would always drive a Packard. But when the car was wrecked and he discovered that the car manufacturer had gone out of business, he bought a Desoto (which also soon went out of business). He wasn't short. And he didn't drive slow. As if he were in a patrol car, he'd gun that sedan up to 50 between the stop signs at the end of each neighborhood block.

"Babe didn't seem to mind Flora's words, because her dialogue about very masculine, female characters was equally pointed: "Now, now, my pet, you know how men are. That's why we ladies understand each other so well. Why we have things to talk about and know how to connect in bed."

"The basis for these novels was never purely imaginative. There was always some story from the newspapers or spotted in a tabloid in the grocery store that they agreed to explore. It was this aspect of writing that intrigued me. First, because they believed they were uncovering the unknowable by use of their intuition, and second, because I knew I could examine what they wrote and, using my intuition, discover a hidden truth about them."

The small servings of bisque were tomato-y with pieces of celery and cut mushrooms. It was so peppery I felt my sinuses open. Kim dug spoonful after spoonful from her cup. Above, old-fashioned ceiling fans turned slowly. There was a low din from other people sitting at tables.

"But there were other things going on at my life at the time.

"I had recently recovered from scarlet fever. This took me out of school for almost half a year. During that time I was in bed, listening to the radio, drawing cartoon strips, reading anything I could get my hands on. I don't know if it was because I was lying down all day and drifting in and out of naps, or because of the fever, but when I did go to sleep for the night I would have strange dreams. Sometimes they seemed unrelated to anything in my life, but at other times it was almost as if I were visiting places, like my classroom or the drugstore on the corner of the large intersection three blocks away, and I was both there and not there—a kind of ghost. I remember once dreaming I was in the basement of Aunt Flora's house. It was after midnight and she was shoveling coal into her old-fashioned furnace. Blades of flame leapt out with every shovel-full. She had a bandana tied around her head, and suddenly she turned and looked over at me in the corner. Her eyes glowed like embers. She raised the shovel over her head, like she would to kill a mouse, and started to walk toward me. I woke up, drenched in sweat."

Kim excused herself, and after asking directions of a woman bussing the tables, went downstairs to use the restroom. The soup had been really salty, so I waved our waitress over. She was wearing a black t-shirt decorated to look like the front of a tuxedo with bow tie. I ordered two glasses of ale. I was sure Kim would be thirsty too but I couldn't see her choosing a dark stout. When she returned I went on.

"Later that month Dan and Babe drove with my great aunt and great uncle to Las Vegas.

"On the way there my Dan's Packard ran a light and they were hit by another car. Great Uncle Charlie was killed. They returned and Great Aunt Annie faced a life of being alone. After I had heard about the accident I saw it in one of my dreams."

"Great Uncle Charlie was Dan's uncle?" Kim asked.

"Right."

"Go on."

"I was almost better by summer. The worst thing about all of this was having to go to the doctor's office each week for a blood test. Even now my veins are difficult to locate under the skin of my arms, and I remember it was an ordeal back then often requiring several tries. School was over for the year, so for my first outing in nearly half a year I decided that on Saturday afternoon I would bike the eight or nine blocks over to see my aunts.

"I walked my bike down the driveway and leaned it up against the fence along the alley by the garage. Then I walked back up to the front screened-in porch and rang the doorbell. I was surprised when it was Uncle Dan who came to the door. He smiled and invited me in, waving toward the outdoor-furniture love seat with woven metal back and hard plastic cushions. He had a glass of whiskey in his hand.

"'Can I get you a ginger ale, Max?' he asked. I noticed he had not shaved in several days which was unusual for him. "My Aunt Annie is sleeping upstairs, and Babe is out somewhere, so let's sit out here."

"'Sure,' I shrugged.

"Dan disappeared into the house and a minute later emerged

with a glass of ginger ale and coaster. He was smoking a Pall Mall. I noticed his drink was now full too.

"'I suppose you heard about old Uncle Charlie,' he started.

"'Yes,' I said. I didn't know what to say, really, and Dan seemed somewhat distracted.

"'I understand you've been sick,' he finally continued, though without much enthusiasm.

"'I'm better now,' I said, thinking that coming here had not been a very good idea.

"Uncle Dan had a flat Irish nose and blonde hair combed straight back like that famous Dan of the time, the movie actor, Dan Duryea. It was strange to see him unshaven and not meticulously dressed. Theirs was an impeccable household where everything was always in place. Perhaps their lives had been this way too. Now, all of a sudden, they were not.

"'We were only one day away from Las Vegas. It had been a good trip. Uncle Charlie was sitting up front next to me but on the passenger's side. I don't know, there just didn't seem to be any traffic at all. Not like Chicago. In any case we had had an early start, before 7, had stopped for breakfast and later for lunch. It was about 3 in the afternoon, and hot.'

"'But you had air conditioning in the Packard?'

"'Yes, that was on, but it was still warm. We were anxious to be in Vegas. I guess I was too anxious. I thought I could make the yellow light. It was out in the middle of nowhere. That's what I was looking at, that traffic light. I didn't see the car coming through the intersection. He must have been going 80 miles an hour. He had the light, I don't deny that. It had changed. And then bang, we were spinning around in circles. When the car stopped. I couldn't believe I was all right and your aunt and my aunt were crying and screaming from the back. I knew they were all right. And I was all right, as I said. And then I looked over at Charlie. His head had cracked the windshield and he was slumped over, his head bent down. He wasn't moving and I knew it was all over.'

"Uncle Dan recited these words to me as if he had said them before. And it wasn't like he was really talking to me, but rather repeating them to himself. I took a sip of ginger ale. The ice cubes clinked against the glass. There was silence. And then I said words that I'm amazed at even today. It was totally untrue. I looked at Uncle Dan and quietly began.

"'Several weeks after Mom told me about the accident I had a dream. And in that dream Uncle Charlie came to me and said something that I want to tell you. He stated that he was OK. He said that before he died he had discovered that he had cancer and that it couldn't be treated. He told me that had he not died in the car accident he would have suffered for many months. He was more afraid of suffering than of dying, and, as it turned out, he was spared from that.'

"Whether or not Uncle Dan believed me, he nodded his head as if he did. Somehow the very possibility of what I was saying made him feel better. Or maybe it was that I cared enough to try and ease his guilt."

Kim said, "You were like a writer telling a reader what he needed to hear."

"I guess so. Yes."

The Safe House was now almost empty.

I leaned across the table and said, "Later that year Dan was assigned to guard the stage door of the Auditorium, downtown. When I next saw him he handed me some glossy pictures of Jerry Lester and the blonde bombshell, Dagmar, personally autographed to Max Jordan."

Night Ten – Grace

Jack Lehman

Chapter 10

Grace

A half hour earlier we had been in the Zen Gallery examining some surreal diptychs. I felt the back of Kim's head lean into my arm as if drifting off in sleep. I turned and look into her eyes. They closed and then opened but did not return my gaze. The collection of paintings on exhibit was titled "Into Shadows, Into Dreams."

The goose a woman was holding in one canvas was straight-necked straining to see something in the adjoining framed picture. In another there was a glimmering spot, globe-like, or like the moon through the wrong end of a telescope. No...on closer examination it was the upside-down painted reflection of two people on the pupil of a huge eye staring out of a painted fog at us. Our reflection?

Later, in the micro-brewery Kim had listened to my long answer to her question about how I had become a writer. But, curiously, she didn't seem at all moved by what I said. In fact now she seemed coldly inquisitive, as if she questioned the veracity of my story.

"And after your Aunt Flora died, what happened to your Aunt Babe?" she asked.

"I last saw her a couple of weeks ago propped up in bed like an aging Mae West, the sounds of the hospital coming through the open door, my windbreaker draped over the back of the uncomfortable visitor's chair. Dan was gone. Flora and her boarder, Nell, my father and mother, and my wife had all gone too. There didn't seem to be much of anything left for me, and now Babe, this mountain of life, was dying.

Kim nodded and took a sip of her ale. I went on.

"This was at St. Francis Hospital located in Evanston.

"I know it. A mammoth yellow brick building with a drive-up under a huge hotel-like marquee. It looks like it would be more at home in Miami or Los Angeles."

"Exactly, Aunt Babe was on the fourteenth floor. It reminded me of the old Edgewater Beach Hotel on Lake Michigan. What a nice illusion. As if dying were checking into a luxury hotel for a vacation."

"And did you ever ask her why she and her sister had not gotten along?"

"I did. That day. She looked at me as my clients sometimes do when I ask them about work they've had done by previous agencies. It wasn't whether or not I would understand their choices, but whether I was worth the trouble of an explanation."

"And?"

"She didn't answer my question. Instead she asked about my divorce. I told her that Carolyn and I just didn't seem to have much in common. It wasn't that we fought about what to do or argued over money. We had settled into a comfortable routine of each doing our own thing. And then, I guess, Carolyn just asked herself, if that was the case, what were the advantages of even being together."

"So you left her or she left you?" Kim asked.

"Technically she left me. But you know how it is in marriage.

"Was there another man or woman?" Kim continued.

I closed my eyes. How did this happen. I was telling her about my aunt and she was questioning me about my life. For several reasons this made me uncomfortable. I went back to the original topic.

I said to my aunt, 'You still haven't told me what it was that caused you and your sister to feel the way you did about each other.' And she replied that she didn't feel strong enough to go into all that. "But," she added, "if you really want to know…"

"'I do,' I said.

"'Then read the story Flora and I wrote together called *Swimming by the Cemetery*." With that she closed her eyes.

"The next day I was told she had died. A week later I got a call from the attorney handling her will, who said I was welcome to go over to Aunt Babe's house and take any keepsakes or furniture I wanted before the estate sale the following Sunday. The proceeds from the sale would be added to the amount I'd inherit as her remaining relative. I thanked him. He told me the key would be left inside the back screen door in an envelope with my name on it.

Early that evening I went to the house."

"And what did you find?"

"It seemed strange to drive my car around back instead of peddling my bike there, but I no longer lived blocks away. Now it was miles. I retrieved the key, which was for the front door. As I reached the top step to the screened in porch, I turned and faced my Aunt Flora's rambling yellow house across the street. There was a wrap-around front porch, and I noticed a child's bike there. I turned and unlocked the door to Babe and Dan's house.

"Their screened-in porch was the same as I'd always remembered it. I entered the main part of the house. The carpeted staircase to the left, the living room with a full mirror over the mantle on the far side to the right. It was dusk and I didn't turn on any of the lamps. Why? For one thing when I was a child everything had seemed new, but with Babe's declining health a close examination of the blue chair and ottoman, the coffee table with dated magazines, even the full length Persian carpet, showed they were worn, dusty or needed a good vacuuming. What had been treasures I was admonished to treat like museum pieces were now junk.

"I walked through the dining room and the kitchen quickly and then retraced my steps to go upstairs. There was only one thing I was interested in, and it wasn't furniture or keepsakes. It was the manuscript of *Swimming by the Cemetery*.

"That's what I was looking for in Aunt Babe's dresser moments later. My uncle and aunt's bedroom stretched across the entire front of the house. It had a formal upright armoire for him and a rounded lower dresser with a large framed mirror for her. At the end of the room stood a high bed with quilts and multiple pillows. To its side, on a metal stand, an old Sylvania Television. I pulled open my aunt's dresser drawers one at a time. There were slips, blouses, pairs of socks, folded slacks and even a small box with jewelry, but no papers."

"I guess that's what you could expect in an elderly woman's bedroom," Kim said.

"Yes. But by now the interior of the house was almost dark. Perhaps she'd converted the extra bedroom at the back to some kind of an office/study. I opened one door and it was the large bathroom lined with black tiles. The next was a closet of shelves with sheets, blankets and extra pillows. Then the back bedroom where I had once slept. I flipped on the overhead light to see better. The room was exactly as I remembered it: a small bed with a yellow satin bedspread, ancient reading lamp next to it and an old photograph of the three sisters and my grandmother on the wall. My grandmother was prematurely white-haired as her children would become. Even I had noticed some strands of white in my hair. I'd come back for this picture. Four women in a world of men. None of my father's brothers who had ventured to Chicago after he had, lasted more than a couple weeks. They were guys who lived for hunting and fishing. Men who never read or spent time with their sons or daughters. They could build sheds, re-shingle a roof, till the garden and listen to baseball on the radio. It was then that I realized my uncle's revolver had not been in the dresser where I had seen it as a child. Perhaps after he died, Babe got rid of the things that were his life. Now I was getting rid of the things that were hers. Just as some day, when I died, someone would be going through my things.

"You are a liar," Kim suddenly spit out at me. "You lie and then you lie and then you lie some more."

I couldn't believe what I was hearing.

"Your mom didn't kill herself; she died of old age. And you and Carolyn aren't even divorced."

I sat dumbfounded. "What do you mean?" I said.

Yesterday, after your call, I talked to Mel Lawton, my boss. He phoned your former employer, Charlie, and we went over to see him. He explained everything, and I felt like such a fool to be taken in by all your stories. Max, I loved you, or could have. Why would you do such a thing? The only reason I agreed to meet with you today is I want you to tell me what is real and what you made up. I want to know why you did it, and, after you tell me, I never want to see you again."

So I told her. "There was no Harry Davidson, I admit that. Oh I did have two warring aunts, and as a kid I could never figure out their relationship, so I made up some reasons."

"And one the aunts recently died? What about the inheritance, is that real?"

"There may be some money, yes. And you have to realize that

Carolyn and I are separated, but because of the inheritance, she now is moving really slow on the divorce. She wants half of whatever it is. I...I just couldn't go into all this, so I made up this guy to not only explain why these women didn't get along, but why I might not end up with much money."

Kim looked at me. Her eyes seemed on fire. Suddenly she squinted and leaned even closer to me. "And what about the manuscript?"

"That's a lie too. I wrote it. I confess. It was stupid. Stupid! But it was something for you and me to work on together. Kim, my life was falling apart. I'd lost my job. My marriage was over. My favorite aunt had just died..."

"You made it up? You wrote the whole thing?"

"Yes."

"I can't believe this. Max Jordan you are a..."

"...writer?"

"You are a complete shit. I can't believe I was so taken in. Was any of it true at all?"

"Most of the details were. The Rockdale part, my mom and her mother and sisters coming to Chicago. My dad."

"How could you pretend your mother killed herself, when I find out from your boss she didn't?"

"Kim, listen to yourself. Isn't that what you were doing with your mom, really?"

"So is your mom alive or not?"

"No, she died, of natural causes several years ago. But I could never figure her out. That's why I wondered if possibly there wasn't something else. That could explain the tension at home. Maybe it was because there was some secret involving her sisters. A secret that explained why their mother had whisked all of them off to Chicago so hurriedly."

Kim thought about her own family. About the alternative wife and daughter her Chinese father had created. As a child she had imagined she was to blame for her parents' unhappiness. Maybe she surmised, I felt that way too.

"That's why I wanted to go with you to your mother's place. To see how someone else's mother might treat her estranged child."

"I don't know what to say," Kim uttered, shaking her head and scooting out of the booth. She pulled her sweater from the coat hook on the pole at the end of her seat."

"I'm sorry. Sorry about everything," I replied. I got up too and we both went toward the front door.

Outside the summer was over. It was still warm but there were colored leaves on the sidewalk and on the trees. We walked toward the parking garage next to The Safe House. Neither of us said anything more.

In the elevator, I pushed the second floor where she had said her car was parked. My old Cadillac was up on the roof.

We both got out on two. I walked behind her to her yellow Subaru. She unlocked the door and got in without so much as a backward glance toward me. After she backed away, I leaned up against the waist-high parking ramp wall and looked at the brick of the building next door. In one sense it was a relief that the truth was out. What had I expected? But now there was nothing. A brick wall.

I felt the car keys in my pocket and swung around. I didn't bother with the elevator, but walked up the stairway the two remaining flights.

When I reached the roof, there were only one or two cars by the stairs. I had parked at the far end, because the length and width of the old Coup de Ville took more space than the markings indicated for a single parking spot. As I turned I saw another car was next to mine—Kim's yellow sedan. My walk turned into a run. When I arrived by the cars she switched off the engine and got out.

"Don't get your hopes up, Mister Writer," she said smiling. "First thing we're going to do is get into my car and drive over to see Grace."

"Who's Grace?"

"Grace is my mother. I think I've cleared her up on who you really are, so this time, I hope, she doesn't beat the shit out of you, like the last visit. Though God knows you deserve it."

Jack Lehman

Day Six – Truth

Jack Lehman

So, Max tells Kim that he became a writer by lying to his uncle, though his intentions were genuine. We listen to this with detachment, but then he admits that he has turned around and done the same thing to Kim (and to us as readers). The foreshadowing helps us accept his deceit as an unreliable narrator, yet we are glad he is caught, and in the last chapter, forgiven.

The story of the two aunts was based on my own experience (Though my aunts weren't writers, I did meet two sisters in Boston who reminded me of them and despite obvious animosity between them they did write mystery stories together.). The incident with my Uncle Dan's car crash that killed his Uncle Charlie, was true. I remember how devastated he was. At the time I didn't know what to do. Fifty-five years later, in a story, I do.

I love the confrontation between Max and Kim. That moment of truth. This release is something I hope the reader feels too. For one thing it accounts for all the discrepancies. It looks back over the parts and this time presents them in a way that not only makes sense but holds together. That sense of symmetry might be the completeness we look for that we don't get in real life—and there is something in us that makes us believe it is possible, if only we could put the clues together.

We leave with this, but also with a deeper understanding of Max and Kim. Their experiences (real or imagined) impact upon them and on us in a way we can't totally dismiss as manipulative. What makes something a classic is its correspondence to the needs of the age. Things go in and out of fashion even though the words might not change. The question is, Do they speak to who we are and what we are going through right now? If they do we honor them; if they don't, they are forgotten. And I think the best way to make this meaningful is for the reader to take a hard look at himself or herself. What are the hurts, fears, risks, inspirations....

I wrote this novella, *The Geography of Sleep*, originally as a stand-alone novella. I had written two others I envisioned as parts one and two of a trilogy. But I was having difficulty with the final one so I decided to convert this separate story into the first of the three Max Jordan novellas.

The set-up was easy enough. I needed to get him from Chicago to Madison (I live in Rockdale). He returns to Chicago in what is now the third book, *Wolves Beneath Chicago*, but the second, *Man with One Ear*, takes place in Madison.

But there was still one piece of the puzzle that remained an enigma: Why Max's mother seemed distant from her sisters? The solution was to write an epigram that promised more books and put the final wrap on this one. That is what follows.

Night Eleven – Epilogue

Jack Lehman

Epilogue

When my mom had died, she'd looked like pictures I had of my grandmother. During one of my visits to Babe in the hospital years later, my aunt recalled when she was young she had gone to a playground with my mother who was watching Flora and her.

"Ruth was older than we were. When we were young she was a stand-in for our mother. She took care of things like banking or servicing the car. For this reason your mother always seemed distant and authoritarian to both Flora and me.

"Once, when your mom was watching us at the grade-school playground, in an unusually reflective moment, she told me and Flora something very personal. The three of us were sitting on a mound of grass off to the side of the swings. Ruth had on a white summer dress, I remember, with puffy, short sleeves.

"She said, 'When I was around your ages I came here with Mom. I had on a swimsuit because it was a hot summer afternoon. She noticed the red birth mark on the back of my left shoulder and said, 'I don't remember that,' and for days afterward I had this strange feeling that I didn't belong in this family, that I had been switched with some other baby at the hospital when no one was looking. Later I read that this is something elves were supposed to do, switch an elfin baby for a human one in the middle of the night. This 'changeling' is then raised by humans who never know this has happened, yet suspect something is not quite right.'"

"'So you're an elf?' Flora asked putting exaggerated emphasis on the 'f.'"

"Your mom answered, 'No, no, it's just that sometimes I do feel I don't belong the same way you two do, that's all.'"

After Aunt Babe's funeral and my divorce, I drove up to Wisconsin, alone. Kim and I had parted on good terms. In fact, we'd become good cell-phone buddies. Anyway, I visited Rockdale, where my parents had come from and even stopped in at Grandma's old house, now The Night Heron Bed and Breakfast where I spent the night. There, in that house, I dreamt I heard those four women talking in another part of the B&B and went from room to room but their voices always seemed to be coming from somewhere else. In the dream I couldn't understand almost any of what they were saying no matter how hard I tried, but once I distinctly heard one of them utter my name.

In any case I left Rockdale and drove 30 minutes over to Madison, Wisconsin, where I decided to stay. With the little money I did get from Aunt Babe, it was a nice place to start over. I even found I could make a living as a copywriter. "Max Jordan, Free-Lance Copywriter." I liked the ring to that. Oh yeah, and I still had a preoccupation with mysteries. Who would have guessed?

My heroes are those private detectives by Dashiell Hammett, Raymond Chandler, Mickey Spillane and Ross Macdonald. They are able to figure out clues and the answers to things. Oh, how I wish I could do that.

Day Seven – But Not Least

Jack Lehman

Writing a novella is great. It may not make much money, but it doesn't cost anything compared to producing a movie or launching a Broadway show.

What about readers? Don't forget you are the first, and maybe most important reader of what you write, though I am a big believer in sharing what we do because it shows, through reactions, that others feel as we do, and encourages us to go even deeper next time—not for fame and fortune, but to live our life more fully. That is Grace, the real "Grace." And your having it does not prevent another writer or any reader from enjoying it too.

Not that there aren't some tricks of the trade. Watch someone pick up a book in a bookstore or library. They look at the title, the front cover, the back cover and if they open it up and like a paragraph or two (start with a scene), they've bought the book.

Pick four or five titles for your book that are memorable and try them out on friends. Don't feel your titles have to label the contents. Most people selecting the book haven't read it, but something in the title clicks for them. *Men are from Mars, Women are from Venus* confirms what most people suspect: males and females are inherently different. The book didn't say much more than that, but sold millions and was the basis for a bunch of sequels.

Get a good tag line: "Writing a Novella for the Digital Age." This not only distinguishes you from the competition but is the fifteen-second elevator pitch publishers can give to distributors who can then repeat it to bookstore book-buyers. Use it in every query letter, or even casual conversation until it feels second-nature.

"What are you working on now?"

"A book called *7 Days and 11 Nights*. 'Writing a novella for the digital age.'"

Gather blurbs from acquaintances. If you feel these aren't enough, go to a book reading and tell the author what you are doing. Then ask if he or she would say something about this. Once I had a book of poems that I wanted an outside editor to look at. I contacted a woman who wrote a poetry column for the *Boston Book Review*. She said, "Sure, I'll do it and I teach at Yale and ordinarily get $2,000 for something like this." About ten times the return I expected on the book, so I said, "How about I narrow the focus down to some specific questions I have and give you $200." She said. "Fine." But the best thing was I got a sentence from her, with her credentials, about the manuscript that my publisher could put on the back of the book. Most writers are sympathetic to those starting out and will help whatever way they can.

Give your chapters, enticing titles. These techniques not only grab a reader's (editor's, publisher's, book buyer's attention), they set expectations and play on natural curiosity.

So what are you waiting for? Stop reading and get writing. You've got seven days and eleven nights.

Write!

ABOUT THE AUTHOR

Jack Lehman is a nationally published writer, poet and playwright. He is a graduate of the Great Books Program at Notre Dame University and has a Masters Degree in Curriculum Development from the University of Michigan. Lehman is founder and original publisher of *Rosebud*, a magazine for people who enjoy good writing and he is the literary editor of *Wisconsin People & Ideas* as well as publisher of the Kindle pulp-fiction magazine, *Lit Noir*. He's the author of six collections of poetry *Shrine of the Tooth Fairy, Dogs Dream of Running, Shorts: Brief Poems of Wonder and Surprise, Acting Les*sons and *The Village Poet, To the Movies*.

His nonfiction books include *Everything Is Changing, America's Greatest Unknown Poet: Lorine Niedecker, Dancing Moon Chronicles, Downward Facing Dog* and *Waiting for Dharma*. His six plays/dramatic readings are: *A Brief History of My Tattoo, The Jane Test, The Writer's Cave, The Last Day of the Sixties, John Jumps* and *Bragging Writes*. They have been presented in Milwaukee, Madison and Saint Petersburg, Florida. His novels, short stories and CDs are on Kindle or in "hard" form available through Amazon. He has been nominated for the *Pushcart* prize in fiction, non-fiction and poetry and is the winner of the prestigious Christopher Latham Sholes Award from the Council for Wisconsin Writers. For more information about him, check: www.LehmanInfo.com.

www.ingramcontent.com/pod-product-compliance
Lightning Source LLC
Chambersburg PA
CBHW060506030426
42337CB00015B/1763